RESURRECTING THE IDEA OF A CHRISTIAN SOCIETY

RESURRECTING
THE IDEA OF A
CHRISTIAN SOCIETY

R.R. RENO

REGNERY
FAITH

Regnery Faith™ is a trademark of Salem Communications Holding Corporation; Regnery® is a registered trademark of Salem Communications Holding Corporation

Cataloging-in-Publication data on file with the Library of Congress

ISBN 978-1-62157-349-4

Published in the United States by
Regnery Faith
An imprint of Regnery Publishing
A Division of Salem Media Group
300 New Jersey Ave NW
Washington, DC 20001
www.RegneryFaith.com

Manufactured in the United States of America

10 9 8 7 6 5 4 3 2 1

Books are available in quantity for promotional or premium use. For information on discounts and terms, please visit our website: www.Regnery.com.

Distributed to the trade by
Perseus Distribution
250 West 57th Street
New York, NY 10107

CONTENTS

INTRODUCTION

Our country is entering a crisis. The once expansive, confident American middle class is dissolving. Economic globalization has eroded the wages of middle-class workers. An ever-cruder mass culture normalizes dysfunctional behavior. People are either winners or losers, and there's less and less in between. We're either climbing to the top of the global economy or sliding down into demoralizing low-wage jobs. Everything, it seems, is fluid, mobile, and impermanent.

I have a young friend whose father has worked his whole life in a steel mill in Gary, Indiana, living for decades in the same house with the same wife. My friend has done well as a software engineer, and one of his brothers has risen even higher in finance. His two other brothers are recovering drug addicts and fathers of illegitimate children. These brothers and their divergent paths reflect our crisis. The stable ground is disappearing. You're either going up or going down. The upshot is widespread unhappiness. Even the successful are consumed by a spirit of anxious striving. Too often despair overtakes those struggling, stumbling, and falling behind.

We can talk about the resulting economic inequalities and the human costs of moral disintegration. I have something to say about both in this book. But the crisis is deeper; it can't be captured in the statistics of drug addiction and suicide. It's a crisis of declining trust and stability, lost solidarity and permanence. We Americans like to compliment ourselves for our independence and self-sufficiency. But there's a dark side to our national character. A deep sadness comes when we realize, finally, that we're on our own, which is where secular individualism brings us in the end. Many now live without a Father in heaven. Political correctness denies them the patrimony of a workable cultural inheritance. For an increasing number of young people, there's not even a father at home. A nation of orphans, literal or metaphorical, will not long endure.

It was against the background of a very different crisis that T. S. Eliot wrote *The Idea of a Christian Society*. Originating in a series of lectures delivered at Cambridge University in March 1939, the book was drafted when Nazism had secured total domination in Germany, fascism ruled in Spain and Italy, and communism controlled Russia. It seemed as though the liberal democratic project had run its course, superseded by more up-to-date ideologies that could forge masses of men into powerful movements and vast armies. Turning back these threats would require tanks and airplanes, strategic planning, and the mobilization of entire nations. But Eliot saw that a more fundamental response was required as well—a decision. Would the West seek a Christian future or a pagan one?

We face a similar decision today. Will we seek to live in accord with the idea of a Christian society, or will we accept the tutelage of a pagan society? Our crisis seems less dire than that of Eliot's day, but we should not underestimate the dangers we face. Democracy requires civic solidarity, the shared sense that we're all in this together. As economic and cultural transformation splits our society into unequal parts, it's difficult to affirm our solidarity anymore. We're disintegrating into two increasingly estranged classes: a super-successful elite and the rest, many of whom lead troubled lives and are dependent on government assistance to get through life.

I'm not a prophet, but I sense that we're leaving behind the democratic era and heading toward a meritocratic one. A meritocracy justifies the wealth and power of its elite on the grounds of their competence and achievements rather than on popular assent. At best, well-meaning technocrats keep the economic machine humming, distributing the material goods of an advanced industrial society and providing therapeutic assurances of "inclusion." More likely, perhaps, is a darker future. Social Darwinism may return, this time in a libertarian guise. "Opportunity" becomes the watchword, and the "losers" in society, their failure self-willed, are thought to "deserve" their place at the bottom. When a culture of freedom becomes a cult of freedom, injustice, suffering, and social dysfunction get explained away as "choices."

The cult of freedom lacks the theatrical bombast of Nazism or the theoretical relentlessness of communism. We do not worship Blood, Soil, or the Proletariat. The idols on offer are softer and smaller. They are the smiling hearth gods of postmodern materialism—health, wealth, and pleasure. They provide the ideals for today's elite: he who is slimmest, richest, and drinks the best wine in the most luxurious private jet wins! And these gods seduce today's losers, whose "bad choices" lead to death from drug overdoses, adult-onset diabetes, violence, and other afflictions of the growing underclass.

This need not be our future. We can make a choice about choice. We can encourage the kind of freedom that serves a higher good. We can opt for the idea of a Christian society. It won't be the one Eliot described but one suited to our own time. I hope we make that choice. America needs repair and renewal, which in our age means restoring a sense of stability and collective responsibility.

In *The Idea of a Christian Society*, Eliot took a formal approach, trying to outline the social structures necessary for Christianity to provide a foundational influence. I take a more concrete approach, tailored to the unique circumstances of early twenty-first-century America. The leitmotif throughout these pages is the need to restore genuine freedom. By my reckoning, a false view of freedom as unimpeded choice and self-definition has led to a deregulation of culture more consequential than market deregulation. This deregulation has benefited the strong and hurt the weak. I outline how and why the seemingly innocent expansion of lifestyle choices has been so harmful. Today's progressivism is waging a war on the weak. Putting an end to that war is the most important social justice issue of our time.

We also need to recover solidarity, limited government, and a sense of the transcendent. These are natural goods that one finds in many cultures. Christian societies do not have a monopoly on them. But ours has been a Christian history, and it is by a renewal of Christian influence that we are most likely to restore these humanizing qualities to our society.

Serving those most in need and contributing to the restoration of American society requires us to speak clearly, honestly, and forcefully. Being a serious Christian does not automatically make one a social or religious "conservative," but the logic of faith runs counter to the cult of freedom. The freedom for which Christ makes us free is quite different from the freedom championed by modern liberal culture, the freedom of self-determining, even self-defining, choice that ends up paradoxically reinforcing our slavery to worldly powers. It is a fundamental principle of the common good that Christian freedom grows in proportion to our obedience to Christ and to the natural truths of the human condition. A society encourages human flourishing to the degree that the supernatural authority of God's revelation is proclaimed and the natural authority of his creation sustained.

This does not mean "establishing" Christianity but speaking up in the public square *as Christians*. We need to say, out loud and with confidence, that we're best off when we live under the authority of the permanence of marriage, accept the duties of patriotism, and affirm the supernatural claims the church makes on our souls. We're "judgmental" not to sustain the preeminence of Christianity in American society, and certainly not because we want to make people feel guilty, but because we seek to promote the wellbeing of our neighbors, especially the weakest and most vulnerable. God's Word judges us stringently. We are to feed the hungry, welcome the stranger, clothe the naked, and visit the prisoner. For what we do to "the least of these my brethren," says Jesus, we do to the Lord himself (Matthew 25:40). It's a sobering warning, one that requires us to look beyond ourselves—beyond our charmed circle of friends—to consider the needs of others. Today's poverty is spiritual and moral. What's needed is the stability and permanence of moral truth, as well as a renewed sense of the possibility of a faith that brings us into the everlasting household of God.

There is much talk among Christians these days about a pessimistic withdrawal from public life. The current of culture seems to be running against us. We need to be realistic about the challenges posed by the present age, and we certainly need to repair our communities of faith. There can be no Christian society without vital churches. But let's not sell the public potency of

Christianity short. The renewal of our society as a whole is possible, even today, even in a hyper-individualistic society like America.

America is full of people who sense the poverty of our postmodern paganism. Our nation is still capable of caring for the weak and vulnerable. Most Americans want everyone to flourish—together. And they don't want to be swallowed by the administrative-therapeutic state, ruled by a remote meritocratic elite. They want their children to seek higher things, the surest way to escape the cult of freedom that makes them servants of today's materialist hearth gods.

Our fellow citizens recognize the seriousness of our faith—loyalty to God, no less! They intuit that we can contribute something solid, enduring, and reliable to public life. It's not going to be easy. But America is demoralized right now. Anti-establishment politicians win widespread support. A wave of populism is demolishing longstanding political coalitions. Polls reveal a dwindling of trust in mainstream institutions. Universities are terrorized by political correctness. Secular progressivism rules our culture more by default than because of widespread conviction. What seems like an all-powerful secular consensus actually churns with dissatisfaction.

Which is why, in this time and in this place, a relatively small number of Christians can inspire and reinvigorate the public imaginations of the disoriented majority. We can renew our society by restoring our voices as Christian citizens.

Resurrecting the idea of a Christian society is possible, but by no means inevitable. The United States is a great nation. I'm a proud patriot. But America is a nation of men, not the city of God. Yes, we may fail to restore the Christian leaven in American public life. It is also true that there will be a time when America is no more. Yet the Gospel endures. Let us therefore take up our political tasks with cheerfulness, even if the odds are against us. We are called to do what we are able, not to succeed. Let's do our best, trusting in God's providence and confident in his final victory.

CHAPTER 1

THE NEED FOR A CHRISTIAN SOCIETY

G etting rich is not the American dream. That's a cliché that tends to be affirmed by immigrants who come seeking a better life for their children. They've yet to be seduced into a genuinely American way of thinking about life. It's also something rich people are inclined to say, which is understandable. Having chosen the enterprise of enterprise, they want to compliment themselves for having achieved our collective ideal. Mammon's slaves naturally assume everyone worships Mammon.

It's true that the vast majority of Americans want to be successful, secure, and financially independent. This requires making money, often a great deal more than one's coal-mining grandfather or floor-scrubbing mother made. And luxury tempts us all. Who doesn't want to be rich?

But the plutocrat is not the American ideal. George Washington was a wealthy man in his day, but we don't revere him for that. Instead, we admire his selfless commitment to his country. The American imagination is captivated by the frontiersman, the cowboy. He's not rich, he's free. We admire inventors for their inventiveness, young men who make their own way in the world. Thoreau in the woods is our romantic hero, not J. P. Morgan in a walnut-paneled office. "Show me the money!"—there's not an ounce of revolution in that Hollywood slogan. "Don't tread on me!" "Live free or die!" "I am a Man!"—those are cries that have led men to take up arms. They've turned the world upside down.

The true American dream, the dream of freedom, has a metaphysical cast: Nobody's destiny is fixed at birth; the future is ours to make. The most famous American of the eighteenth century, Benjamin Franklin, was the quintessential self-made man. Our metaphysical dream has an economic side, true. Being born poor doesn't doom you to remaining poor. Franklin went from a penniless youth to great wealth. But there are many other sides to that dream. Each of us is free, and that freedom is more important than a big bank account. The lament of Orson Wells's character in *Citizen Kane* expresses a wholly American sentiment: "If I hadn't been rich, I might have been a really great man."

To be American is to dream this dream of freedom. It's been my dream. One evening decades ago when I was working on an oil rig on a remote butte in south-central Wyoming, as the sun was sending its final light across the open landscape, I stood next to Julio, my Mexican coworker, looking out over a vacant Highway 287 stretching south to Rawlins. He sighed with deep satisfaction, "Life is good, my friend." Good not because we were making a lot of money during the late 1970s oil boom, though that was good too. Good because he and I and the rest of the crew worked in splendid, superior isolation, five men drawing from the depths of the earth the lifeblood of our industrial age. Everything seemed possible. Distant mountains turned red, then purple, in the invading darkness. In that moment, as in many moments on that rig and throughout my life, the world seemed open, ready, mine.

Yes, it's my dream, this American one. But I know it's heretical. This world is God's, not mine. It's not for me to make myself into whatever I wish. God, not my sovereign will, is the Supreme Being. In him we live and move and have our being.

This metaphysical dream of freedom is false to reality as well. As a boy, I used to play basketball with some of the students at my grandmother's school for mentally retarded children. I had my dreams of freedom, but their destinies were largely fixed at birth. The same was true for the black kids from inner-city Baltimore who attended my church's summer camp. To some degree we're all mentally retarded and from troubled backgrounds, but our DNA, our families, our schools, and our communities equip some of us more generously than others. A high IQ is given, not earned. The same goes for acquired characteristics like self-confidence and self-discipline, which are nurtured in us by others. When somebody praises me for a good work ethic, he's indirectly praising my parents. Our very existence is entirely the doing of our parents. No one is a self-made man.

Yet I still believe in the self-made man! My American dream fixes on freedom's promise. Why? Why in spite of what I know to be true?

Perhaps it's because our Puritan forebears would not allow the failures of the Christian past to limit their vision for a Christian future. Or because our country was founded by revolutionaries who shrugged off the old ways of the Old World and founded a new order for the New World. Or because for so long our nation opened out onto what seemed a limitless western frontier, where there was always a place to begin anew. Or because so many generations of immigrants cut the umbilical cord to family and homeland. Or because our long national ascent to global supereminence has given us a sense of an ever greater future.

Whatever its sources, the fact of the American dream of freedom is plain. The myths of self-reliance and destinies self-made that inspire us are no less powerful for our recognizing them as myths. To believe my destiny is my own to make is a one-sided exaggeration, a dream more than reality. But it's our American genius to be encouraged as long as we recognize at the same time that freedom flourishes only when it serves.

DEMOCRACY AND FREEDOM

The democratic revolution that defines the modern era—a revolution more of the imagination than of the mechanics of government—has transformed American society more than any other, our constitutional checks on majority rule notwithstanding. In his famous invocation of the ideal of democracy, Abraham Lincoln referred to "government of the people, by the people, for the people," meaning not the Anglo-Saxon people or the Irish people or the African people. That would be a government by the *peoples*, in which the public space is divided among various ethnic groups, an arrangement in accord with the ancient vision of empire, not a democratic society. Lincoln meant simply *the people*, without distinction of racial or ethnic or cultural identity.

Thus the essential ideal of the democratic revolution: government for the sake of *everybody*. To most of us, the notion is uncontroversial, but from a historical perspective it is indeed revolutionary. From time immemorial, politics and group identities—the *peoples*—have been intertwined. Democracy breaks with that pattern, rejecting a social order defined in terms of *peoples*. The vote of an aristocrat counts for no more than the vote of a laborer. The child of an immigrant has as much right to public office as the scion of a *Mayflower* family. The American dream is that my destiny—at least in its public, political aspect—is not fixed by my birth. The *peoples* do not control my future.

Like all revolutionary projects, this ideal has an aggressive side. It demands the uprooting of the political and cultural traditions that categorize persons according to their place among the *peoples.* Unlike France, America had no aristocracy to put an end to. We had slavery instead. Lincoln insisted that the purpose of the Civil War was to preserve the Union, but it was precipitated by a fundamental dispute about the legitimacy of slavery, and it quickly became clear that the full power of the federal government would be used to destroy the institution of race-based slavery. Nearly all whites of the time, even those committed to the abolition of slavery, assumed the inferiority of blacks, yet the war was fought to ensure that this view would not be allowed to justify slavery or any other systematic subordination on the basis of race—a profound expansion of the scope of freedom. The logic of the war was the logic of the democratic revolution. If a black man is free to make his own way in life, *anyone* can be free. In this sense the Civil War was the "re-founding" of our country, a "new birth of freedom."

Yet there is a paradox. How do we get from government of, by, and for the people to freedom? If rule by the majority is the essence of democracy, what becomes of individual self-determination? Wasn't the North's refusal to accept Southern secession and its enforcement of political union by military conquest a denial of Southerners' freedom to go their own way?

In fact, the democratic ideal and an individualistic view of life are two sides of the same coin. We can govern for the sake of all—*the* people—only if we challenge and dethrone the power of the *peoples* to shape our destinies and control our lives. The Civil War was fought to enforce the principle that our ethnic, religious, racial, and class identities must not be the basis for the laws of our society, and the Fourteenth Amendment was passed to codify that principle. Government by one of these *peoples* would not be government by *the* people.

Democracy, therefore, distinguishes between me the individual and me the member of a community. Justice is supposed to be blind to my ethnic, class, and racial identity. If I'm tried for a crime, my family background or ethnicity shouldn't be evidence of my guilt or innocence, nor should my vote be magnified or diminished by my place among the *peoples*. In the eyes of the state, I'm an individual, not a placeholder for a group or representative of others.

We take this legal and political individualism for granted. But the democratic ideal can transform culture as well, and in America it always has. We're strongly disinclined to accept the class-based cultural and political distinctions that until recently were characteristic of European countries. Our social imaginations are democratic. We're to make our way as individuals, free of the life-determining power of group identity. We want a culture of the people, by the people, and for the people, not defined by white European traditions, male preferences, or any other form of group identity.

This has turned out to be very difficult to achieve, although our distinctive national history can make us think otherwise. For a long time after blacks were accorded a degree of equality before the law, it was still assumed that they were rightly subordinate to whites. Among whites, the descendants of the original Anglo-Saxon settlers saw themselves as a natural aristocracy, and men from that ethnic group thought it quite natural and proper to assume the most prominent roles in a social system that was anything but democratic. In economic competition and the closely related competition for social status and political power, blacks had no standing, Jews were outsiders, and swarthy Catholic immigrants were regarded as dangerous aliens. Women might be white, rich, and upper-class, but they were discouraged, and in some cases prohibited, from competing with men for professional status and public roles.

In the second half of the twentieth century these social inequalities came to be seen as intolerable, and a series of social revolutions attacked the perennial human tendency to sort people according to their tribal affiliation. The most dramatic of these was the civil rights movement, which was part of a larger campaign against formal and informal caste systems in American society. We're now unwilling to presume that Italians hold *this* sort of job and that Jews hold *that* sort, or that women should play *these* roles but not *those*. The goal has been to promote a social freedom commensurate with the political freedom guaranteed by the Constitution. In all our social interactions, not just in our relation to the state, we're to be treated as individuals.

As the democratic ideal expanded from the voting booth and the courtroom to every aspect of life, the American dream came to encompass something unprecedented in human history: a *culture* of, by, and for the people. The resulting cultural revolution has, like the Civil War, destroyed and driven to the margins the culture-shaping power of traditional forms of social authority that have been organized around race, ethnicity, religion, and sex.

The most successful front in this revolution has been the effort to stamp out racism. The average American in 1950 could scarcely imagine today's mixing of blacks and whites. Bill de Blasio, New York's white mayor, his wife, Chirlane McCray, a black woman, and their two biracial children represent a profound and unprecedented transformation. The same is true of countless unions of Asians and whites, Jews and gentiles, Hindus and Christians. In the past, marriage and family, the foundations of any strong communal identity, were always carefully guarded, and few married outside their group. Today, by contrast, we have an increasingly democratic culture of marriage. Approaching it with our individual needs and desires in mind, we consider our potential partners as individuals, not as Asian or white or Jewish. This extraordinary new freedom to marry whomever we wish, along with the remarkable (if incomplete) success in overcoming old patterns of racism, encourages us to imagine even more dramatic transformations. If the power of the *peoples* can no longer limit our most intimate choices, why should our bodies? If the American dream is true, if my destiny is truly mine to make, nature herself must be shouldered aside.

The feminist movement of the second half of the twentieth century rejected the view that a woman's sex should determine her standing in society, launching a cultural revolution that is ongoing. We feverishly teach young people not to adopt sex-based expectations about anything. A woman can kill on the battlefield while a male nurse tends the wounded. A man can stay at home and take care of the babies while his wife closes deals at work. The logic by which this attitude seems to follow from a culture of, by, and for *the* people explains why the women's movement easily draws upon the civil rights movement for inspiration and rhetoric.

A unisex culture might be logical, but it's also unnatural and therefore more difficult to achieve. We're powerfully inclined to sort human beings into male and female categories, an inclination that evolutionary biology suggests is wired, unlike racial or ethnic or religious sorting, into our brains. That's a serious impediment to acting as if male and female were arbitrary social constructs. But the powerful myth of freedom is now driving zealous efforts aimed at reprogramming. When President Obama visited a charity that delivers toys to poor children at Christmas, he made a show of putting boys' toys into the girls' bin. When questioned, he replied, "I'm just trying to break down these gender stereotypes." He was acting in accord with our dream of freedom: nobody's future should be constricted by expectations about what it means to be a boy or girl. Nothing determines our destiny, not even our biology. Our futures must be ours alone to make.

This vision of freedom drives the campaign for ever-expanding gay rights, a campaign that might shape the American dream as decisively as the Civil War did. A person's sex should not limit his choice of sexual partners, nor should he bear any civil or social liabilities on account of his sexual choices. And now that gay rights has won the field, the campaign has been expanded to "transgendered" persons, who insist that one's anatomy should not determine whether one lives as a male or a female and that the choice itself can even change from day to day.

If we step back, that's a very odd thought. I don't think any of the pioneers who fought for equal rights for women three and four and even two generations ago would have thought our chromosomes are irrelevant to whether we are male or female. It certainly would have struck Martin Luther King, Jr. as very strange. But the logic is irresistibly appealing to those bewitched by the American dream. If we really can live in a way free from our maleness and femaleness, then the horizon of our freedom is almost limitless. Why should my future be limited by my body's subjection to disease and decay, any more than by my nature as male or female? I fully expect that within a few years academics will advance the view that mortality, like sex, is socially constructed. Such a view provides the anti-metaphysical foundation for a right to doctor-assisted suicide, euthanasia, and abortion. I can easily imagine the argument: There's no such thing as death; it's a construct imposed on us by traditional ways of thinking that sustain the interests of the powerful.

Perhaps we recoil from the extensions of freedom that deny all limits, even to the point of denying reality. I certainly do. But they follow from our metaphysical dream of freedom when it loses touch with its metaphysical underpinnings. Think about it. Our dream of freedom promises that no man's destiny is fixed at birth. Why, then, should nature dictate? Why should genitalia dictate? Why should our decaying bodies dictate? Why should DNA dictate? Why should *anything* other than freedom alone, operating in a void, govern our futures? Unless we're ready to propose an end or purpose for freedom to seek and serve, we'll end up saying that freedom is for the sake of freedom. The American dream thus turns into a totalitarian nightmare of political power marshaled to subdue *everything*—except freedom.

EQUALITY AND FREEDOM

Freedom, which is at the heart of the American dream, should not be confused with equality. If blacks have lower incomes than whites, if they are less likely to attend college or attain high social standing, then we assume they have less freedom. We assume the same about women with respect to men, and so on. We make equality a test rather than a goal. Unequal outcomes suggest unjust infringements of freedom.

Social programs promoting equality cater to this view of freedom. We're told we need to expand access to resources so that more individuals can make their own destinies. In American politics, redistribution is rarely promoted for its own sake. All the talk about income inequality today reflects a worry that some people aren't getting a fair shake. It's a concern about freedom, not equality—or perhaps it's more accurate to say it's about equality for the sake of freedom.

There is a desire today to redistribute more than economic resources and educational opportunities. Many want to "redistribute" social status. They think it's damaging for schools to publish class rankings, for example. Every child participating in a running race gets a medal. The motives here are complicated, but it's thought that if young people see themselves as losers, they'll internalize low expectations that will undermine the full exercise of their freedom as adults. Equality is a means to protect the American dream of freedom.

It's tempting for conservatives to see multiculturalism as the product of Marxism, but that is a mistake. Multiculturalism is best understood as an egalitarian cultural therapy. The curricular decision to sideline "dead white males" and highlight minority writers is the cultural equivalent of the progressive income tax that funds a substantial income supplement for the poor. The dominant white male has to take a back seat so that others can have their time at the wheel, but the goal is not equality. Women and minorities receive special encouragement and opportunities for cultural expression so they can find their own "voices." Far from an anti-American perversion, multiculturalism serves the American dream—everyone must have the greatest possible freedom to make his own future. Every cultural barrier must be dismantled! It's not surprising, then, that multiculturalism is more virulent in American universities than in European ones.

As an educational ideology, multiculturalism does more than empower minorities. If that were its sole purpose, the white elite in America would resist it. Yet they warmly endorse multiculturalism because it caters to *their* dream of freedom as well. It puts everyone on the same plane. The Chinese have their way of thinking. Muslims have theirs. We have ours. The same goes for high and low culture. You can study Milton or comic books, Shakespeare or sci-fi films.

This pedagogy dissolves culture's claims on us, discouraging us from thinking that one way of living is better than another.

For many critics, this approach to education is horrifying. No way of thinking is superior to any other? If that's true, then there is no truth, which is nihilism. But this dour assessment misses the moral purpose of multiculturalism, which reflects the American commitment to freedom above all else. For if one way of thinking is as good as another, then all of us are freer to choose how we wish to think and thus how to live! We can mix and match, as New Age religions often do. Or we can make our own experiments in living. A white male cherishes this freedom just as much as anyone else, which is why he endorses multiculturalism even though it seems to cast him as the "bad guy" in so many narratives of oppression.

Critics often point out that multiculturalism is inconsistent. It insists that all cultures are equal but denounces Western culture as uniquely oppressive. But the anti-Western tenor of multiculturalism expresses a profoundly Western ambition, one born in the democratic ideal of the modern era. More than two centuries ago, men asked why being born a peasant ought to dictate one's role in society, and they demanded political freedom. The same was true of their social roles, and they demanded freedom from all caste systems and rigidly fixed social roles. Now we find our universities full of people who question why the happenstance of being born in the West should dictate their moral convictions. If my destiny is not determined by my social class or race or religion or even my body (the focus of the sexual revolution), why should it be determined by my culture? If we prize the dream of freedom above all else, the most American thing to do is to renounce the authority of Western culture!

Anti-Americanism is thus a kind of hyper-Americanism, something I fear most American conservatives fail to recognize. A repudiation of America strikes a blow for still greater freedom. If we take America down a notch or two, we disenchant the inherited social norms that control us, giving ourselves psychological space to live according to whatever values we prefer.

If we think this way, then being anti-patriotic is the highest and most noble way to be patriotic. If this seems paradoxical, recall that Thomas Jefferson mused that it would be good to have a revolution every twenty years, and Ralph Waldo Emerson viewed society—*American* society—as an enemy of self-reliant freedom.

Moral relativism, closely related to multiculturalism, is promoted as a cognitive therapy that enhances freedom. Young people are taught to be nonjudgmental, to let others live as they please rather than according to an established moral or social script. Educators who adopt this approach don't see themselves as nihilists. On the contrary, they're proud of the moral purpose of their work, which is to ensure that the next generation has the freedom to define morality for itself. This moral purpose—serving the American dream of freedom—explains why moral relativists can be so judgmental, ferociously denouncing the view that marriage is the union of a man and a woman, for example, or that certain sexual acts are immoral. The moral relativist is defending freedom, the freedom to define moral truth for oneself.

What are we to make of the strictness of moral relativists' views about smoking, recycling, and global warming? There is no contradiction. They object to certain behaviors, but they base their judgment on scientific considerations of health and sustainability unrelated to the internal moral norms that shape one's sense of self. The moral relativist does not seek to undermine the pragmatic conditions necessary for a well-functioning modern society. Nor does he question the deliverances of scientific authorities. The goal of moral relativism is to secure for us an internal freedom to determine moral norms for ourselves.

Many conservatives denounce multiculturalism and moral relativism, and rightly so. Many have reservations about gay rights. Still others regret the way in which feminism has demolished courtship and poisoned male-female relations. These are all legitimate responses. I share them. But we need to understand that these developments have sprung from the American dream of freedom. If our governing ideal is the American dream of freedom, then why not celebrate those who break their ties with their male and female bodies? Or those who break their ties with Western culture? Or those who toss out the distinction between good and evil? If freedom alone is our watchword, how we can object?

FREEDOM'S TYRANNIES

Taken in isolation, the American dream produces the conditions for ever larger government, more coercive laws, and a culture of denunciation and censure that limits freedom, though always for the sake of a supposedly greater freedom. This tendency toward tyranny becomes more evident as our democratic ideal turns toward the transformation of our culture, as it has done since the 1960s. The leading edge of progressivism now seeks freedom from human nature itself, a goal that fosters a Jacobin spirit determined to destroy all that stands in the way.

We may dream the American dream of freedom, thinking of America as a place where every individual is free to make his own destiny. But in politics some are freer than others. Liberals accuse conservatives of being lackeys for corporate interests, while conservatives accuse liberals of serving the interests of the technocratic class. We may want a government of the people, by the people, and for the people, but we're constantly worrying that these people or those people, this group or that group, controls the levers of power. Our worries are well founded, for the reality is that some people have greater resources, and thus a greater say in public affairs, than others.

And so the American dream of freedom inevitably contradicts itself: We must deploy the coercive power of government to promote freedom; we must limit freedom for the sake of freedom. Recent debates about campaign finance regulations provide an example. Recognizing that wealth amplifies an individual's voice, we feel compelled to intervene. The liberal, who wants to use the regulatory power of government to limit the role of money in politics, seeks to restrict how much money individuals can contribute. The conservative rebels against limiting freedom for the sake of freedom, arguing for full disclosure rather than funding limits. If everyone knows who is funding whom, an informed citizenry will use its vote to check the undue influence of money on politics.

The conservative case for disclosure and against strict regulation would seem to be freedom's obvious agenda. What could be more burdensome to freedom that intrusive government regulations? But as the American dream has evolved over the past century, our concern about government constraints has waned, and we have focused instead on how our material and social conditions limit our futures. If we're to have government of, by, and for the people, then everyone ought to have the *same* power to influence public policy. The happenstance of my poverty should not limit my freedom in this regard, just as the happenstance of another man's wealth should not enhance his. Conservatives are loath to admit it, but the logical outcome of this way of thinking—which stems from our very American view of freedom—will be the liberal view taken to its logical conclusion. The little guy can be truly free to influence public policy only if we prohibit campaign contributions and provide public funding for all political activity. Government must eliminate private advantages and disadvantages to ensure equal freedom for all.

The analogy to today's cultural politics is not hard to see. Just as every citizen should have an equal freedom to influence public policy, so he should have an equal freedom to influence cultural norms. Why should a white, straight male American have more cultural influence than someone whose background puts him on the periphery? Isn't a democratic culture one that is of, by, and for the people, not one dominated by this or that sector of society? In pursuit of such a culture, progressives engage in something like campaign finance regulation writ large, demanding "inclusive" approaches that limit the voice of once-dominant groups and re-allocate cultural authority to the formerly voiceless. This cultural "affirmative action" seeks to make everyone equally free to influence our public culture.

The dictatorial multiculturalism at today's universities is shallow and oppressive, but we need to be honest—it follows from our myth of freedom. If our destinies are not fixed by what we inherit from our culture or our parents, why should a young black man from a poor urban neighborhood raised by a single mother face lifelong limitations? We understand *why* his destiny is severely constrained—poor education, lack of good male role models, violence, crime, and so on. But nearly all Americans, conservative or liberal, agree that our society would be *more* democratic if his future were as open as that of the most privileged child. The same goes for a young woman. Why should her prospects in life be more limited than her brothers'? And what about men who want to have sex with men or women who want to have sex with women?

So our dream of freedom encourages ever more dramatic interventions. Think of all the circumstances that shape us: social norms, family background, and the limits imposed on us by nature. Compared with political oppression, which the democratic project has done a great deal to overcome, this kind of cultural, even natural, enslavement to the conditions of our birth requires powerful tools of liberation, often very powerful tools.

Some of those tools were forged during the civil rights era. The Supreme Court's decision in *Brown v. Board of Education* (1954), the Civil Rights Act of 1964, and the Voting Rights Act of 1965 gave the federal government extensive legislative and executive power over southern states, allowing it to set educational policy, rewrite voting laws, and arbitrate the drawing of electoral districts. Laws against discrimination in housing and employment produced unprecedented federal intervention in economic and social relations. These laws were then elaborated and extended by various regulatory agencies. At the same time, a powerful cultural movement led by schools, churches, and the press drove supporters of racial discrimination from polite society.

William F. Buckley, Jr. and others warned that a full implementation of the civil rights agenda would dangerously increase the power of government. Since racism penetrates to the most intimate dimensions of life—that's why it is so pernicious—uprooting it requires an exceptionally intrusive application of the power of law. Buckley and the conservative critics were right, of course. Civil rights legislation amounted to a massive government intervention in economic and social life and the most extensive experiment in social engineering ever undertaken in America. The effort has been largely successful, and Buckley eventually acknowledged that it was necessary, admitting that his earlier resistance to a full-scale, government-led assault on racism had been mistaken.

But he was not mistaken about the role coercion inevitably plays. Once created, the legal and social machinery for eradicating racial discrimination was available for other causes, in particular the women's movement and sexual liberation. In defense of individual freedom, the government now intervenes against the once universal belief that the natural differences between men and women should have moral and social consequences. The courts have expanded their dominion to the point of redefining marriage and the family, and progressive cultural forces gather their strength to reeducate us, monitoring our every word and act.

The women's movement may have reached a limit. Most Americans, including women, haven't wanted to eliminate all distinctions between men and women. Even so, implementing women's liberation has required more coercion than was necessary to secure civil rights for black Americans. However pronounced America's racial divisions were, they were limited, for the most part, to the surface of society. Before the civil rights movement, there were interracial romances and marriages, as well as integrationist movements and institutions that refused to conform to racist principles. By the middle of the twentieth century, moreover, American segregation, like South African apartheid, was an anomaly. When James Baldwin moved to Paris in the 1950s to escape from American racism, he was treated as exotic, not inferior.

By contrast, most of our inherited attitudes toward intimate and domestic life assume the male-female difference. The ideology of sexual equality, if taken to the extreme, repudiates that difference and requires the dismantling of much of our traditional culture. The gay-rights movement also rebels against the male-female difference, requiring, in turn, an even more extensive reengineering of traditional culture.

Again, we need to be honest with ourselves. These liberation projects are consistent with the American dream. They're also consistent with a powerful, coercive government. Two centuries ago, when political freedom required the destruction of the premodern social-political system, the French revolutionaries, having seized the power of the state, swept away the *ancien régime*. The sexual revolution has likewise made full use of the powers of the state, along with relentless social stigmatization, to destroy the public power of traditional moral norms.

None of this should come as a surprise. Unchecked by loyalty to God, nature, and custom, the American dream of freedom cannot help but become militant. The future is mine to make! I can be anything! There's nothing about the accident of being born into Western culture that can control my future! I'm even free from the maleness or femaleness of my body!

The promise of life without limits intoxicates. If I can dismiss my body, then perhaps I can be free from the reality of death itself. This dream of an ultimate freedom, freedom from death, helps explain why transgender rights have become so important. Advocates speak of a "gender *assigned* at birth," insisting that such an assignment should not limit a person's freedom to decide if he's male. The notion that my maleness is *assigned* at birth is pregnant with the promise of immortality, for the mortality of my body has an even greater claim on me than the body's maleness or femaleness. Perhaps we'll soon speak of the "mortality assigned at death." To a certain degree we already do. It's called a right to doctor-assisted suicide, the triumph of freedom over mortality by *willing* one's death rather than *suffering* it.

Our freedom is terribly fragile. The days I spent at my grandmother's school for mentally retarded children taught me that. No matter what the activists say, our bodies are not assigned at birth. They develop from our DNA, itself a legacy of a long evolutionary process. Securing a total freedom—always only for the sake of freedom—will require us to criminalize nature. This is impossible to achieve, of course. Nature resists arrest. But if today's ideologues of freedom have their way, we will have to endure a long season of totalitarian efforts to do what can't be done.

FREEDOM'S FOUNDATION IN LOYALTY

We need not travel all the way to freedom's totalitarian dead end. Freedom properly understood is based in a pledge of loyalty, not a declaration of independence. Our country's freedoms arise from eternal verities affirmed, not ties severed. As the Declaration of Independence says, "We hold these truths to be self-evident." The first and fundamental act is *holding*, not *choosing*, standing fast in truth, not making it up. We are freest when we acknowledge the authority of the truth, not when we seek a godlike independence from all limits.

Authority is not the same as power. Power compels by force, while authority directs our lives because we assent to its commands. When football players trust their coach, they accept the plays he calls on the sidelines, not worrying over his reasons. They assent to his authority as the play-caller. But in assenting, they take responsibility for executing the play. In their obedience to his authority, it becomes *their* play, an expression of their freedom made all the more powerful by the coordination of their individual wills toward a single purpose. This is possible only because of the coach's authority.

Political philosophy calls this fusion of the power of command with free assent legitimate authority. In its most effective forms, legitimate authority issues commands we accept and internalize, taking responsibility for pressing them forward, improvising, and even criticizing for the sake of achieving the commanded goal. True patriotism is not a passive disposition of nationalistic pride. It's an active loyalty, addressing defects and seeking to purify and renew a shared heritage.

If we see authority as illegitimate, however, conformity to it grates. We feel commands as a kind of bondage. What we are required to do is at odds with, or at least unrelated to, what we hold to be true. We submit, perhaps. Governing authorities have great power, after all, and they can threaten us with penalties and punishments. But our obedience is not free.

In traditional cultures a conflict between illegitimate authority and freedom is largely accepted as part of the brokenness of temporal life. Christianity emphasizes the need for free assent to the highest truths of faith, but it has nevertheless taught submission to political authority, even if it is unjust. We may not actively assent to injustice or do evil willingly; Christianity guards the integrity of conscience. But in many circumstances we must offer "passive obedience," as it is called, to incompetent, ineffective, venal, and unjust authorities. We freely work out our salvation before God in fear and trembling, but before the magistrate we're to grit our teeth and largely do as we're told.

Rejecting passive obedience, the democratic ideal makes legitimate authority essential. As Lincoln's definition of democracy stipulates, we seek a government of, by, and for the people. All of public life should be a zone of free assent, or at least as much of public life as possible. A truly democratic nation aspires to be a football team, collectively agreeing to the coach's play calling. As the great Enlightenment political philosopher Jean-Jacques Rousseau put it, ideally, the will of every individual is perfectly aligned with the "general will." In the perfect democracy, what every individual wants and what society demands are one and the same.

This ideal has been realized to a striking degree in many Western democracies. In our own country we have hard fought, sometimes bitter electoral battles. We feel there's a great deal at stake, and often there is. I can testify that I'm often not pleased with the laws emanating from Washington. I strongly dissent from the reigning interpretation of the Constitution that imagines it provides women with the right to abort an unborn child.

Nevertheless, there are very few of us who don't wholeheartedly assent to our constitutional system, taken as a whole. Consider the 2000 presidential election. Who *really* won in Florida: Bush or Gore? A narrow five-to-four vote by the Supreme Court, on partisan lines, provided the legally binding answer, and nobody took up arms. Later, many people criticized Bush's policies, but only those on the fringe denounced his presidency as illegitimate. For all intents and purposes, what Rousseau had in mind is found in America. We have a regime that enjoys a super-consensus of support.

But this alignment is not perfect, which is why there's a temptation to solve the problem of legitimate authority by individualizing it as much as possible. This was Ralph Waldo Emerson's insight. Like Rousseau, he sought the perfect union of commandment and freedom. To ensure this outcome, he stipulated that the only commandments we should obey are those we give to ourselves. This approach guarantees legitimate authority from the outset. Freedom obeys only freedom.

That's our problem, today. When "Obey only yourself!" becomes the first and greatest commandment, freedom undermines itself. The tight end's freedom is fullest—he can exercise his will most effectively to overcome that which impedes his ambitions—when the first and greatest commandment is thou shalt obey thy coach and the second is like unto it, thou shalt serve thy teammates. That's even true for solitary endeavors. No self-trained athlete runs a four-minute mile.

In fact, freedom's need for authority is so great and so fundamental that without it we suffer some of our most painful experiences of limitation. I might have been drafted into the army or debilitated by a severe illness. Either situation would have impeded my efforts to be a good father. Yet when I look back on my life, I find myself regretting the inconstancy and conflicting desires that led me to spend time on things that seemed more important than my children. The impediments thrown up by my undisciplined, disordered soul bring the deepest regrets. So when I hear someone say, "Be true to yourself!" I shake my head. It's bad counsel. I have failed precisely insofar as I have been loyal to myself. As a father, I needed to be delivered from my weaknesses, not encouraged to obey them. That's possible only if a voice of command comes from the outside. To be free to achieve our most cherished goals we need authorities we can trust, assent to, and make our own.

The same is true for America and our collective genius for freedom, which should be redeemed from its excesses rather than rejected. We cannot use freedom alone as a sword to cut the bonds of race, class, sex, or anything else. If we try, we'll end up in the cruelest bondage of all, which is to ourselves. A voice has to come from the outside. Freedom comes when we bind ourselves to something worth serving. Martin Luther King, Jr. recognized this in his letter from a Birmingham jail, an evocation of the double-barreled authority of America's founding principles and God's revealed word. A culture of freedom requires legitimate authority. Freedom is fullest not when it serves itself but when it serves truths freely held. We need to resurrect the living power of the truths undergirding our society, many of them Christian truths, if we're to restore and renew the American dream of freedom.

When Pontius Pilate interrogated Jesus, he knew the prisoner's reputation. Some of the Jews in Jerusalem were hailing him as their long-promised king. This amused the Roman governor, for Jesus was under his dominion. Pilate had the power to sustain his life or decree his death. Pilate questioned him, "Are you the King they desire?" The response Jesus gave was nothing less than a provocation: "You say correctly that I am a king. For this I have been born, and for this I come into the world, to testify to the truth. Everyone who is of the truth hears my voice." In all likelihood, Pilate was taken aback by this arrogant response. But he gathered himself and asked the question we've all heard in our relativistic age, one meant to stop conversations and forestall the emergence of legitimate authority: "What is truth?"

When faced with freedom's failures, we half-know that we need something other than a closed-circuit idea of freedom for freedom's sake, freedom as a self-chosen destiny. We half-know, because as we've destroyed every claim upon our destinies other than freedom's empty promise, our lives have become poorer not richer, more vulnerable not freer. We need loyalty to sustain our liberty. The cowboy isn't free because he's free. He's free because he cherishes his honor above his paycheck, his vocation above society's fickle acclaim. The red-streaked sunset moves his heart more than calculations of self-interest; a higher loyalty gives him a place to stand. In order to be free we need a higher truth to serve.

What is truth? Jesus does not answer Pilate's question. Neither do I. I can only describe the idea of a Christian society, a national culture not dominated by Christians but leavened by them. Perhaps Christ's truth is not *the* truth. Perhaps the voice we need to harken to is the Buddha's or Mohammed's or some yet-to-be-born prophet's. There is peril in obedience ventured. The authorities we affirm may prove false. But of this I am convinced: we must take the risk. Our American dream of freedom will become a nightmare if we do not put it in the loyal service of something greater than ourselves.

CHAPTER 2

DEFEND THE WEAK

Post-industrial America is a good place for the well educated and the upper middle class. Economic globalization has expanded entrepreneurial and investment opportunities. The wealthiest sliver of the population's share of all income earned has risen substantially as tax rates have dropped. But the past fifty years have not been good to those with only a high school diploma. The globalization that has done so much for the professional class has undermined the working class. We've all heard about the rise in income inequality. In his surprise bestseller *Capital in the Twenty-First Century*, the economic historian Thomas Piketty offers statistical evidence that we live in a new Gilded Age dominated by a super-wealthy class, the "One Percent."

Piketty's statistics have been rightly debated, as have his speculations about the laws of capitalism. But something just as important, perhaps more important, doesn't get talked about: *moral* inequality. We are living amidst a cultural transformation comparable in magnitude to economic globalization, and it too favors the powerful. Today's "progressive" is committed to expanding lifestyle freedom, which the rich tend to manage, like economic freedom, to their advantage. But while the benefits of economic freedom do in fact extend even to the poor, what trickles down from lifestyle freedom is dysfunction, disorder, and disarray.

The campaign to legalize doctor-assisted suicide promotes death with "dignity." It's a rich man's luxury, a soft landing for the high achiever who's been the pilot of his own life. Someone who's used to getting his way feels entitled to determine the circumstances of his death. It seems a benevolent extension of freedom. Who is harmed? But cultural change affects everyone, and there are costs paid by others. Between 2005 and 2015, suicide among adults age thirty-five to sixty-four increased nearly 30 percent. Oregon, the first state to legalize doctor-assisted suicide, saw the greatest increase—a 50 percent rise from 1999 to 2010. Trickle-down culture can be deadly.

Bill Clinton famously insisted that though he tried marijuana, he never inhaled. What he meant by that comically implausible statement was that he had used pot "responsibly." Educated, well-to-do Baby Boomers are disciplined in their hedonism, careful that their peccadillos don't impede their scramble for success. For the most part, the rich have developed a relatively safe and moderate approach to drugs, and for the few who haven't, well, there's professional help. Decriminalization of marijuana won't hurt the strong. But what about the weak? Kids who use marijuana regularly get lower test scores, are more likely to drop out of high school, and are less likely to go to college. And who are they? A 2011 study reports that children of parents who have not completed high school are twice as likely to smoke marijuana as children of those who have completed college. Again, new freedoms harm the vulnerable.

The talented and educated are enjoying an expansion of their economic opportunities while old moral strictures on their pursuit of pleasure melt away. The American dream seems to be triumphant, at least for those able to take advantage of the new freedoms. Yet the life expectancy for white people without a high school diploma has dropped catastrophically since the 1990s—down by five years for women, three years for men—suggesting a cultural crisis among poor whites akin to that in Russia after the Soviet Union collapsed. Yet the morally preening powerful, confident in their supposedly progressive views, largely ignore this collapse and the people suffering from it. When bureaucrats or journalists occasionally take notice, they offer every explanation except the obvious one: white, secular progressives have dismantled traditional morality, disempowering and disorienting the weak and vulnerable.

Yale University is famous for its Sex Week. It does not have a Dignity of the Worker Week or even a Save the Planet Week.

This self-involved focus speaks volumes about the preoccupations of today's ruling class. Our culture wars are driven by the rich, who insist that our shared moral culture serve their interests by promoting freedoms that benefit them and harm the poor.

No social crisis of our time is more profound than this disregard—to the point of disdain—for the moral needs of the vulnerable. Official ideologies of "diversity," "inclusion," and "nonjudgmentalism" are not oriented toward the "marginal." They serve the high achievers, the meritocrats, the comfortable people who have the social and financial capital to navigate this moral deregulation and protect themselves from its dangerous consequences. The progressive cultural politics on the march today is at odds with the Bible's fundamental social principle: "Rescue the weak and the needy; deliver them from the hand of the wicked" (Psalm 82:4).

THE ONE PERCENT

Charles Murray's *Coming Apart: The State of White America, 1960–2010* is an illuminating account of how the social contract is being rewritten and how the changes have affected the poor. His focus on whites allows him to control for the significant demographic changes in this country since 1960. It is also the case that the American elite, whose progressive cultural politics has altered the moral consensus, is still dominated by whites. There are many stories to tell about America, but this one, the story of white America, is surely among the most important, as Murray recognizes.

The first point to make is obvious. There's a growing economic gap between the rich and everyone else. In the fifty-year period of Murray's survey, annual household income for the top 1 percent grew from $200,000 (in 2010 dollars) to more than $400,000. Household income for the bottom half, on the other hand, stayed flat and would have fallen without redistribution programs such as the earned income tax credit. This divergence is important, but it's not Murray's main concern. Instead, he focuses on the social gap. The saying "the rich are different" has never been truer, and the divide is moral as well as financial.

Notions like "ruling class" are difficult to define. Strictly speaking, the percentage of the population with direct power over large organizations such as major corporations, universities, and government bureaucracies is extremely small, even less than the 1 percent that has been the focus of the debate about income inequality. But an upper-class culture encompasses more than those who exercise power directly. It includes ACLU lawyers who have degrees from elite law schools, as well as college professors, even if their incomes are modest.

Murray opts for a capacious definition of our upper class. In his shorthand, they live in an imaginary town he calls "Belmont," named after a toney Boston suburb full of well-educated professionals. The statistical cohort of Murray's Belmont are "prime-age" (thirty through forty-nine), "have at least a bachelor's degree and are managers, physicians, attorneys, engineers, architects, scientists, college faculty members, or in content-production jobs in the media (e.g., journalists, writers, editors, directors, producers)," or are married to someone who is. This turns out to be about 20 percent of the American population today, our new upper class.

At the other end are the people represented by Murray's "Fishtown," named after a white working-class neighborhood in Philadelphia that has been somewhat gentrified since *Coming Apart* was written. They are in "blue-collar, service, or low-level white collar occupation[s]," hold "no degree more advanced than a high school diploma," and account for about 30 percent of prime-age white Americans. They are the old working class that has become America's lower class, or even underclass, to use a term originally coined to describe black urban poor communities that suffer from crime, low marriage rates, illegitimacy, and intergenerational poverty.

Analyzing changes in Belmont and Fishtown from 1960 to 2010 is difficult because of the enormous social changes in that period. In 1960, fewer Americans went to college, and therefore fewer qualified as Belmont residents—only 6 percent of prime-age adults. Fishtown was much bigger: 64 percent of prime-age white Americans were not educated beyond high school. Murray works some social scientific magic to come up with a plausible top 20 percent (Belmont) and bottom 30 percent (Fishtown) circa 1960, allowing him to proceed with his project of showing how widely society's top now diverges from the bottom.

Marriage, Murray says, is "the fault line dividing American classes." In 1960, white America conformed to the "bourgeois consensus," an overarching moral code for sex, marriage, and family that largely corresponded to the biblical precept that marriage is the only proper context for sexual relations and that its purpose is to provide a stable basis for raising children. This bourgeois consensus was strong in 1960. Transgressors paid a price, sometimes a high one. The censorious atmosphere ensured that the vast majority of prime-age adults in both Belmont and Fishtown married, few children were born out of wedlock, and couples rarely divorced.

Then came the sexual revolution and the women's movement. In 1965, the Supreme Court overturned Connecticut's law prohibiting the use of contraceptives. Though long unenforced, the law symbolized strict expectations about sex, marriage, and family, which is why it was challenged by progressives. The court formulated a right to "privacy" that in subsequent decisions was extended to protect abortion and sodomy. The elite progressives got what they wanted: the old sexual ethic unraveled.

At the same time, no-fault divorce superseded more restrictive laws. There was an explosion of divorce in the 1970s, and it lost its stigma. Premarital sex, cohabitation, and eventually homosexuality became widely accepted, and in 2015 the Supreme Court declared that men can marry men and women can marry women. In what seems like the blink of an eye, the "bohemian consensus," reflecting the values of experimentation and personal freedom, replaced the old bourgeois consensus: consenting adults may have sex whenever and with whomever they wish, while marriage (however defined) and children are optional.

Though the bohemian consensus is now widely shared across social classes, it disguises significant divergences in practice.

People in Belmont teach their children to be nonjudgmental, tolerant, and inclusive, speaking carefully of "nontraditional families" rather than "broken homes," of "single-parenting" rather than illegitimacy. Belmont is the place most likely to endorse gay rights and support "marriage equality." But Murray shows that despite its profession of the bohemian consensus, today's upper class lives in accord with the old bourgeois one.

The numbers are striking. Today, 85 percent of prime-age adults in Belmont are married. That's a decline from the 1960 figure of 95 percent, but a surprisingly small one given how much our moral culture has changed. No-fault divorce has led to an increase in break-ups, but, again, not by much in Belmont, where slightly more than 5 percent of those married have been divorced. Children born out of wedlock? In spite of what we read about celebrities, they're uncommon in Belmont. Members of our upper class may talk the talk of the sixties, but they walk the walk of the fifties. David Brooks, with his usual wit, calls them "bobos," bohemian in attitude and self-image, but bourgeois in behavior.

Meanwhile, Murray's statistical Fishtown actually lives the sixties. They're just plain bohemian, though without the élan associated with self-consciously countercultural lifestyles. Less than 50 percent of prime-age adults are married. More than 35 percent of those who have been married are divorced. Nearly 25 percent of children are being raised by single mothers. Sixty percent of the children of mothers who dropped out of high school are illegitimate (to use that forbidden word). Only 30 percent of children in Fishtown are living with both biological parents when their mothers turn forty.

There's a word to describe this trend: collapse. It affects even those who stay married in Fishtown. Their self-reported happiness in marriage has declined. The culture of marriage in poor white America today is more frayed than it was among blacks in 1965 when Daniel Patrick Moynihan issued his dire warning, *The Negro Family: A Case for National Action.* Worse, the trend lines suggest continuing decline in the future. Given the importance of stable families for healthy, functional communities, Murray warns, this collapse of marriage "calls into question the viability of white working-class communities as a place for socializing the next generation."

There are other signs of crisis. Since 1960, Fishtown males have become more likely to be unemployed, and when they do work they're more likely to put in part-time hours. Back in the 1960s and 1970s, white male working-class unemployment tended to rise and fall with the national unemployment rate, indicating that the main factor was macroeconomic trends. Since the 1980s, however, it has risen even when the national rate has declined, suggesting that more insidious cultural factors are at work. The rate of prime-age white males on permanent disability has also risen, and this in spite of the decline in heavy manufacturing jobs usually associated with disabling workplace injuries.

There is increasing concern about crime and high rates of imprisonment among blacks, but the problem is not blacks' alone. Although Fishtown's rates of crime and imprisonment remain much lower than among blacks, they have increased nearly five-fold since 1970. Meanwhile, crime and imprisonment in the upper class remain minimal. It's still 1960 on the streets of Belmont.

When it comes to church going, it's not 1960 in Belmont, to be sure. Among the upper class 20 percent of the population now has no religious affiliation, the same as in Fishtown. The picture changes, however, if one considers church attendance. Close to 40 percent of prime-age males in Fishtown say they attend church regularly, while in Belmont the figure is 55 percent. This is the reverse of conventional wisdom. The media tend to portray religious belief in decline among elites while remaining strong among less educated, poorer people. That may have been true a generation ago, but the opposite is the case today. Declining religiosity has accelerated among the less educated, while the percentage of religious believers with college degrees has actually increased since the 1990s. There's not just an income gap in America, there's a God gap.

Although women have professional careers and progressive views about sex are *de rigueur*, Belmont residents are neotraditional. They form stable families, encourage their kids to work hard, and are involved in their communities. Meanwhile, the people of Fishtown are post-traditional. To dramatize the difference between these two ways of life, Murray offers some telling comparisons.

In Belmont, less than 5 percent of males between the ages of thirty and forty-nine are not "making a living," which Murray defines as earning enough to keep a household of two above the poverty line (a mere $14,634 per year in 2010), a rate that has been constant since 1960. The men of Fishtown have always been relatively poor and uneducated, but in the 1960s, only 10 percent of prime-age males failed to make a living. Today the figure is more than 30 percent. The problem is unlikely to be ameliorated by an increase in the minimum wage (which might be a good idea for other reasons). Few of those prime-age males failing to make a living are missing the mark because of low wages. They often aren't working at all or are working irregularly. For the bottom third of society, the problem is more a weakened culture of work than low wages.

A second striking divergence between Fishtown and Belmont is in their rates of out-of-wedlock births. That rate has quadrupled since 1960 in Fishtown, but single mothers are uncommon in family-friendly Belmont. Likewise, the rate of "isolates"—people with no civic or religious involvement, largely disconnected from others—has quadrupled in Fishtown since 1960, causing community institutions like the PTA and local clubs to wither. Isolates are rare in Belmont, where community institutions enjoy strong local support.

Taken together, these three demographic categories—men not working, single women with children, and disengaged persons—give us a picture of what Murray calls "dysfunctional people." Fitting into one of these categories, of course, is not necessarily the result of a "failing." There are plenty of single mothers who work hard and raise their children well, and some people are out of work or isolated for reasons beyond their control. But statistics tell an overall story, not personal ones. In the aggregate, men who don't work, single mothers, and the socially isolated are not effective community-builders, or even sustainers. Belmont has only a few dysfunctional people, Fishtown far more, with trend lines going in a bad direction.

The division of white America into two very different worlds, which Murray documents with statistics, is obvious to anyone who cares to open his eyes. There are many good people living in Fishtowns all across America, some heroic in their commitment to their families, some doggedly committed to community orga-nizations, single-handedly sustaining them in difficult circum-stances. But the prevalence of dysfunctional behavior is making it increasingly difficult to enjoy a happy, decent life in Fishtown.

WAR ON THE WEAK

Belmont residents like me work hard to ignore Fishtown. The reason is simple. We don't want to face our responsibility for the destruction of the moral and spiritual integrity of working-class America. We *like* the bohemian moral consensus, which serves our preferences even as it shreds the moral fabric of Fishtown. The weapon of mass destruction in our war on the weak has been moral relativism, heedlessly deployed by an elite culture in love with critical strategies for disenchanting old, inherited moral norms.

Strictly speaking, though, "relativism"—the philosophical stipulation that no moral truth exists or that what is right and wrong is up to the individual—is not the right word to use here. The sort of person inclined to say that morality is a psychological projection of the superego or a patriarchal social construction or the upshot of evolution is also likely to affirm an extensive menu of "human rights," suggesting less a rejection of moral truth than a shift in its focus. It's telling that we call this set of (rigorously enforced) convictions "political correctness" rather than "moral correctness"; it tends to be political, not moral in the traditional sense. So we should drop the term "relativism," which wrongly suggests that in Belmont everything is permitted, and instead adopt "nonjudgmentalism."

The main purpose of nonjudgmentalism is to soften moral judgments that affect us personally, allowing us to make up our own minds about what's right *for us*. A high school student in Belmont, told to make "healthy" decisions about drugs, alcohol, and sex, is encouraged to make his "own choices" and to respect the choices of others. Nonjudgmentalism dismantles "dominant discourses," the sources of confident judgments about what counts as right and wrong.

Nonjudgmentalism is like market deregulation. It is intended to open up formerly regulated spheres of life. Sex is the most obvious of these but by no means the only one. We're to be nonjudgmental about divorce and doctor-assisted suicide—difficult situations, we're told. The *New York Times* might publish a story about a couple who decided not to abort their Down Syndrome child, as long as the writer makes it clear that those who abort their children aren't doing anything wrong. "There are no easy answers."

Anyone who spends time in Belmont knows how powerful this nonjudgmentalism can be. We censure smoking, but that's about physical health. We insist on dramatic social changes in response to global warming, but that's a matter of irrefutable science (or so we're told). In the main, we find it difficult to criticize anyone's personal behavior in specifically moral terms. We may grimace during the summer months at the sight of tattooed women displaying their illustrated bodies. But explicit expressions of disapproval are *faux pas* in Belmont. Perhaps we know a middle-aged father who has decided his lucrative career is no longer fulfilling and has quit to open a bike repair shop. Are we able to do anything other than signal our approval and support, even as we recognize that his self-regard is likely to make his family's life difficult? Don't people have a right to self-fulfillment?

As we deregulate morally, a therapeutic and medical vocabulary takes over. Belmont addresses moral situations with the delicacy and circumspection once reserved for speaking about sex. Euphemisms abound. Small children throw temper tantrums and mothers respond by telling them that their behavior is "unhelpful." A child is caught cheating in school, and the guidance counselor emphasizes that doing so is "unproductive." Drug use is "unhealthy." Parents discipline their children only in the softest, least judgmental terms.

Belmont's nonjudgmentalism allows for new kinds of regulation. Some are explicit. For example, Belmont children are subject to nonnegotiable expectations of academic success far more rigorous and relentless than when I was a child. Admission to elite universities enhances the status of parents and is the gateway to economic success for their children. Other regulations remain unspoken. Belmont parents won't refer to "illegitimacy," but they succeed in socializing their children to marry before having children. Like a community with a private, coded language, upper-middle-class parents discipline their children while outwardly observing the pieties of nonjudgmentalism.

Murray finds the coexistence of official nonjudgmentalism with the strikingly traditional norms of behavior in Belmont "one of the more baffling features of the new-upper-class culture." He shouldn't be flummoxed. Belmont is isolated from the rest of America, as his research shows so clearly. Exclusive neighborhoods, private schools, and elite universities provide a safe environment for experimentation (although the furor over date rape and sexual assault on college campuses suggests that it's not as safe as many imagine). An intense focus on academic and career success builds strong habits of self-discipline. When the nonjudgmental guidance counselor in Belmont affirms the importance of making "healthy choices," she is supported by the ambient culture of achievement that encourages caution and prudence.

Nonjudgmentalism, therefore, works reasonably well for the well-to-do. A recent survey of Harvard seniors shows a low degree of sexual experimentation and cautious drug use. So why moralize? There is, after all, a downside to moral strictness. The people in Belmont are human too. Some get divorced. Some sons are gay. Some daughters are promiscuous. Alcoholism afflicts more than a few. Stigmatizing these behaviors makes for a punitive environment of moral inflexibility. Better to remove the stigma and make the rules more plastic, giving people more room to live as they please. Murray's data show that Belmont uses its moral freedom wisely. What's the harm of nonjudgmentalism? Why force everyone into a single, authoritarian mold? Doesn't a public morality that refrains from strong moral judgments about personal behavior produce a more inclusive, more tolerant society that allows for creative freedom?

Actually, no.

Nonjudgmentalism breeds an inequality more profound and consequential than a growing divergence of income, splitting society into two realms, the functional and the dysfunctional. In the former, governed by discipline and decency, basic social institutions such as marriage thrive, while in the latter the conditions for dignified lives are undermined. Our ongoing insistence on nonjudgmentalism—in spite of the obvious harm it does to the poor and vulnerable—reveals the heartless underside of American society. Even as globalization is bestowing decided economic advantages on Belmont, that same ruling class promotes a public culture that provides its members with moral advantages as well, very much at the expense of the weak.

A brilliant, passionate book written by the British anthropologist Mary Douglas in the late 1960s can help us understand what is going on. In *Natural Symbols*, Douglas studied two systems of authority and social control first identified by Basil Bernstein in the 1950s. In "positional control systems," typical of the working classes, social roles are assigned according to one's social position rather than negotiated. So if my position is that of a father, I must abide by a "restricted code"—that is, I must behave as a father is expected to behave. I must be a breadwinner, for example, and the voice of discipline in the household. A child who grows up in this kind of system develops clear expectations. If a young boy asks his mother, "Why can't I play with dolls?" she provides a straightforward answer: "Because you're a boy." The positional control, restricted code system provides bright lines, clear answers, and little wiggle room. For this reason, progressives attack it as authoritarian, rigid, empty, conformist, and inimical to genuine individuality.

There's a great deal of truth to these criticisms, but they ignore the virtues of a restricted code system. Its clear definitions of a good father, a good husband, and a good worker, its easily identified roles, its simple statements of right and wrong erect a sturdy set of guardrails for society. Yes, this approach encourages conformity, but in so doing it gives people, especially the young, who need guidance, the directions they need for living an honorable life.

The second system of authority and social control that Bernstein identified is found higher up the social ladder. Here parents explain the whys and wherefores of rules. To the question "Why should I do my homework?" there is no set answer. The response might be, "Because your mother and father want you to succeed," or, "Because it's important to live up to expectations," or even, "You need to think about the importance of education and decide for yourself if homework is an appropriate priority for you." As Douglas explains, in this system "control is effected through either the verbal manipulation of feelings [or] through the establishment of reasons which link the child to his acts."

Here we see the source of Belmont's nonjudgmentalism. The personal, enhanced code socializes young people to become active agents in their own moral lives. This was the explicit goal of Lawrence Kohlberg's theory of moral education, which culminates in a "post-conventional" outlook valuing reasons over rules. Kohlberg's theory has been extremely influential, and its authority remains impervious to reasoned criticism. The "post-conventional" moral outlook can be called bohemian, not in the sense of starving artists in Greenwich Village, but in the sense of rejecting the presumptive authority of inherited rules. A bohemian "post-conventional" approach to socializing children will naturally use nonjudgmentalism as a tool for making moral codes more flexible. Children need to be trained to question inherited norms so they can achieve a free relation to their moral inheritance rather than simply conforming to set rules.

This is not to say conformity is absent in Belmont—far from it. Recognizing the need for social conformity, our ruling class today is no more likely to produce radical individualists than was Bernstein's middle-class London society. Deviation from a set pattern of "individuality" is unlikely, as anyone who has spent time at an elite university knows. The goal in Belmont is to blend an appropriate (to use a pervasive weasel word) conformity with genuine (another weasel word) individuality. In contrast to the working-class world, where living an honorable life is for the most part a matter of occupying pre-established social roles, in Belmont a morally successful life is one in which a person develops the verbal skills necessary to manipulate the open-ended, enhanced code. To use Murray's terms, it means being nonjudgmental in a way that confirms bourgeois expectations without giving the impression of being a conformist. The paradox of Belmont's official nonjudgmentalism is that while it rejects old-fashioned moral strictness, it nevertheless demands conformity to 1950s-style bourgeois norms. Everybody is an individual—in pretty much the same way.

As an example of an ill-considered imposition of the personal, enhanced code on the working class, Douglas cited the decision of the English Catholic bishops in the 1960s to lift the requirement of abstaining from meat on Fridays in favor of a discipline personally chosen by each of the faithful. For Irish Catholics in England, Friday abstinence had been an important identity marker, buttressing their sense of cultural integrity in a historically inhospitable Protestant society. The progressive elites of the church, seeking a more "modern" and "intentional" form of Catholicism, heedlessly undermined the system of social control that suited working-class Catholics and gave their lives dignity.

This episode in Catholic life (which had its counterpart in the United States) epitomizes transformation of public culture since 1960. It would be wrong to imagine that traditional modes of life in the West have been entirely about roles and conformity, rules and obedience. One need only consider Thomas Aquinas's method of teaching, which started with reasons to think various Christian doctrines *wrong* and then reasoned out why they are true. Until recently elites raised their children in ways that encouraged a similar effort to take possession of moral norms in a reasoned way. This reflective moment, however, operated within rather than against society's positional designations and restricted codes. For the most part, elite children, even when encouraged to question the rationales for authority, also functioned within pre-established social roles reinforced by clear rules.

I experienced this in my own upbringing. My parents ran an enhanced-code household, to use Bernstein's terminology, but also enforced restricted codes. I was encouraged to think through the reasons for rules, even to contest them—which I did. I argued that wearing a tie to church was empty conformity to an elitist social rule. My father's response: "Clever, and now go upstairs and put on a tie." I was being trained in an old-fashioned way. A reflective life questions inherited norms, much as Aquinas encouraged his students to question. But those at the top of society, who have the luxury of questioning, also have a responsibility to uphold social standards that apply to everyone, including themselves, just as Aquinas thought he and his students were under the authority of divine revelation.

When I was a child, that consensus was already changing. Young men started growing their hair long in a collective rejection of a social code that distinguished between male and female appearances. This transgression was symbolic of a larger rejection of *any* system of positional control. It's not an accident that this trend began in the universities, at the top of society, where it was also accommodated. Nor was it an accident that this symbolic rejection of sex roles was at first fiercely resisted by the working class, as the movie *Easy Rider* dramatized. The hard-hat class knew intuitively that its way of life was under assault, not from below, but from above.

The assault has been ongoing and implicates every aspect of social life. For decades universities have undertaken to reeducate students, trying to get them to avoid any reference to the positional control system that distinguishes between male and female. The efforts go to absurd extremes, regulating pronouns and insisting on coed bathrooms. Today, the unisex "they" has replaced "he" and "she."

This verbal gesture, which is common in Belmont, works in tandem with obligatory nonjudgmentalism. Even today, a working-class woman might speak of "illegitimate children." It's a positional way of talking, one that divides right from wrong, good women who have children in the proper circumstances from bad women who don't. A morally loaded term, it shames deviance and thus reinforces social rules, which is precisely what a mother might want to do to inculcate sexual discipline in her daughters. I'm quite sure, though, that speaking of "illegitimate children" at a PTA meeting would evoke censure from an educational "professional." The working-class mother would be corrected and told she should use neutral terms such as "out of wedlock" or "non-traditional family." In these and countless other instances, repeated over and over again in the past few decades, Belmont-style nonjudgmentalism has become the mandatory approach for everyone, uprooting and destroying older restricted codes and systems of positional control. As Douglas saw, this assault, now well advanced, amounts to a new kind of class war.

"It sounds like this mother's heart is in the right place," explained Kirsten Filizetti, a San Diego psychologist, when asked to comment for a newspaper story about a parent who punished her daughter for cruelly teasing a fellow student. "She was trying to help this girl understand what she had done and teach her a life lesson. However, parents should be careful about introducing shame and guilt onto kids as a form of punishment." The mother should sit down with the child and help her understand and reject the motivations for bullying.

This small, almost innocent, yet typical episode of therapeutic hauteur reflects our society's division by a moral inequality as severe as—and in all likelihood more damaging than—income inequality. The psychologist uses her authority as an expert to undercut a straightforward exercise of parental authority (positional control). She asks instead for a sophisticated verbal exchange between mother and child (personal control). This may be well-meaning, but it is an exercise in class dominance. In the eyes of the elite, with their therapeutic understanding of the human condition, Kohlberg's final stage of moral development is superior, and anyone who fails to attain this stage is, by implication, morally primitive.

It is easy to imagine what would happen if a working-class parent spoke up at a school board meeting against a proposal to teach elementary school children about homosexuality. From their perch on the moral heights, the Belmont representatives would insouciantly dismiss the plebeian protest: "We can understand why you might not want your child to have to talk about sexual orientation. But in Glenn Springs we're committed to creating an open, inclusive environment for all students, and that means being proactive at an early age so that children don't say hurtful things and develop unhealthy attitudes." The enhanced-code virtuosi of Belmont set the rules, denying the basic moral competence of ordinary people.

As this class war makes public culture more and more "post-conventional," to use Kohlberg's term, individual freedom is increasing. What earlier generations took for granted, we must decide. To have sex or not have sex—and with whom, when, and how? To have children or not to have children? What am I supposed to do when I become a father? To marry or not to marry? Do I need a husband to raise my children? Do I need a woman to have children? Should I freeze my embryos? Should I end my life rather than endure suffering? In a post-conventional society such as ours, there is no end to open questions.

Well-educated people are often prepared to deal with these open questions. People who are good at talking tend to succeed in social systems that encourage talking things through. The magazines read in Belmont, like the *Atlantic*, feature articles by Ivy League women about negotiating a world with weak sex roles, few explicit rules for sex, and no settled consensus about whether children are more important than careers. The weekend *Wall Street Journal* publishes columnists who draw on brain science and evolutionary biology to come up with supposedly scientific principles for living well. They are Emily Posts for a post-conventional society, providing the creative class with fodder for its endless cogitations about how to navigate through life without fixed rules and roles.

Meanwhile, Fishtown goes to hell. This isn't surprising. In pursuit of post-conventional freedoms we have destroyed the old systems of positional control, leaving adrift the poorly educated and those who lack the skills to navigate the post-conventional seas. Deprived of normative sex roles, poor people today don't negotiate and renegotiate male and female relations the way upper-class people do. They flounder. Marriage declines. Illegitimacy increases. Male-female relations turn sour.

This class war, a war on the weak, is epitomized in the campaign for gay marriage. There's no more potent symbol of a post-conventional society. Redefining the age-old institution of marriage is in one sense a great achievement for freedom, transforming a once authoritative restricted code—one man, one woman—into something utterly manipulable. Marriage has become another plastic, open-ended option for the upper class. Belmont's ability to sustain marriage in spite of the remarkable transformations of the sexual revolution is well documented by Murray. This suggests that upper-class society will absorb the new freedom of men to marry men and women to marry women without much trouble. The data from Fishtown suggest exactly the opposite. Gay marriage bids fair to be yet another moral luxury for the rich that will be paid for by the poor.

———

On the road to Jerusalem, Jesus tells his disciples the fate that awaits him. Their own dreams of glory make them deaf and blind to the truth. James and John, the sons of Zebedee, petition Jesus, asking to sit on his right and left hand in his glory. In rebuking them, Jesus rebukes all of us who imagine ourselves superordinate, deserving of our superior roles in society as activists, managers, therapists, and right-thinking people who set the tone for everyone else: "You know that those who are supposed to rule over the Gentiles lord it over them, and their great men exercise authority over them. But it shall not be so among you; but whoever would be great among you must be your servant, and whoever would be first among you must be slave of all. For the Son of man also came not to be served, but to serve, and to give his live as ransom for many" (Mark 10:42–45).

These words judge us today. Can we begin to count the academic feminists who demand ever-greater freedom from sex roles? Whose freedom does this serve? Certainly not the men and women of Fishtown. The present concern for transgender rights amounts to a mass hysteria. Normally sane liberals seem unable to resist demands that boys who identify as girls be permitted to use female locker rooms. Again, whose freedom does this serve? Certainly not the men and women of Fishtown. And what about new reproductive freedoms? Surrogacy? Sperm banks? These are preoccupations of the One Percent. The same goes for the new freedom for men to marry men, and women to marry women, or for people to end their lives, or for women to terminate their pregnancies. Today's culture warriors on the left trumpet their commitment to justice, but they lord it over the weak, redefining our public culture in countless ways, claiming to serve the marginalized but always empowering those adept at post-conventional enhanced codes—which is to say, themselves.

A Christian society follows Jesus: the strong must serve the weak. In this service our freedom is perfected. Given the reality of sin, every society will fall short, but we can do better than the relentless war that our culture of liberation wages on the weak.

As Amy Wax, a law professor at University of Pennsylvania, has observed, vulnerable, socially disoriented people often need financial assistance, healthcare, and other social programs. But more than anything they need clear rules that direct them toward decisions that help them lead dignified lives. Nonjudgmentalism, now obligatory, refuses to meet this need, treating clear moral strictures with suspicion, if not outright hostility, seeing in them a dangerous regression to older, "conventional" social norms. It's a mortal sin in Belmont to answer a child's question with a clear answer like "Because you're a girl." You get denounced in public if you describe any sexual act as "unnatural."

A Christian society would encourage us to debate sex roles, what is natural and unnatural, and the norms that should govern other domains of life. There's nothing uncritical about a society committed to strong and clear moral norms. But we can't have a society that serves the weak if we don't end our war on the very possibility of clear rules. There can be no justice if we don't unseat the post-conventional from its position of supreme authority. We need to criticize the critics for their often unconscious but all too real service of the powerful. A Christian society judges nonjudgmentalism unjust.

CHAPTER 3

RAISE UP THE POOR

ore than a century ago, Walter Rauschenbusch
published *Christianity and the Social Crisis*. The
crisis he addressed was caused by rapid industrialization. Workers flocked to the cities, where jobs were to be
found. Older modes of life that once provided ordinary people
security, if not opportunity, disintegrated. Deprived of the
interlocking networks of village life, the urban working class
was vulnerable. Unorganized, they lacked bargaining power
and political clout. Rauschenbusch called for the churches to
respond, not just with charity, important though it is, but also
with political action. He envisioned a political and economic

order based on biblical principles of justice. That program came to be called the Social Gospel, one of the most important Christian movements of the twentieth century.

There is a great deal to criticize in *Christianity and the Social Crisis*. Rauschenbusch's enthusiastic support for social change grew, in part, out of his impatience with the Bible's supernatural claims. It's not Jesus's resurrection that matters, but the political implication of his proclamation of the Kingdom. Nevertheless, there's an enduring truth in Rauschenbusch's formulation of Christianity's social responsibilities. The Bible calls us to raise up the poor. In the era of rapid, unregulated industrialization, that meant defending children against exploitation, supporting unions, prohibiting slumlords from taking advantage of the urban poor, protecting laborers from unsafe workplaces, and more. For all its defects, the modern regulatory welfare state stems from a genuine Christian response to social and economic problems. There are still injustices of these sorts that properly concern us.

Today, however, we face a new revolution, a cultural revolution. Families and communities are under threat, just as they were in Rauschenbusch's day, but now the threat is the new moral outlook of nonjudgmentalism, which, as we saw in the previous chapter, seems to work for people at the top but has been a disaster for the poor and the middle class. The most pressing social justice issue today is the moral exploitation of the poor and vulnerable by the well off and powerful, an exploitation masked by the rhetoric of liberation.

PREFERENTIAL OPTION FOR THE POOR

Rauschenbusch was trying to be faithful to the spirit of the twenty-fifth chapter of the Gospel of Matthew. There, Christians are enjoined to welcome the stranger, feed the hungry, clothe the naked, and visit the prisoner. The Social Gospel was one way to turn this spiritual imperative to care for the least among us into a social ethic. The Catholic tradition has its own approaches. In *Octogesima adveniens* (1971), the apostolic letter marking the eightieth anniversary of Pope Leo XIII's Catholic version of the Social Gospel, *Rerum novarum*, Pope Paul VI recalls the fundamental importance of self-sacrificial love. "In teaching us charity," he writes, "the Gospel instructs us in the preferential respect due to the poor and the special situation they have in society: the most fortunate should renounce some of their rights so as to place their goods generously at the service of others."

In Catholic circles, the phrase "preferential respect" was soon eclipsed by "preferential option for the poor," a term from the "liberation theology" that arose from the crises of poverty and oppression in Latin America. The phrase, which has percolated into many Catholic pronouncements on social issues in recent decades, suggests that when we think about our political, economic, and cultural responsibilities, our first question should be, "What are the needs of the poor?"

There is certainly material want in America today, and the question how to address it drives much of our political debate. Some say the best approach is to adopt tax policies that will stimulate economic growth. A rising tide lifts all boats. Others emphasize private charity, arguing that local institutions know the particular needs of the poor they serve. Still others seek increased government intervention, believing that only the state has the resources to address large-scale economic problems.

Whose approach is best? It's an argument worth having. The moral character of a nation is measured to a large degree by its concern for the poor, and we should affirm a preferential option for the poor. But poverty is not only material; it is also moral, cultural, and religious. It's a sign of the poverty of our public discourse that discussing the moral and spiritual poverty of the poor is positively prohibited. We're not to "blame the victim." And as we have seen, the people of Belmont prefer a moral culture that indulges, licenses, and empowers the rich and powerful, even at the expense of the poor and vulnerable.

This scandalous code of *omertà* is a sad sign that we've become a post-Christian society. Visit the poorest neighborhoods of a major American city or an impoverished rural town and you'll quickly discover a misery more profound and pervasive than simple material want. Drugs, crime, sexual exploitation, divorce, fatherlessness, streams of expletives, pornography, violent images—they are everywhere. The sheer brutality and ugliness of the lives of countless Americans—not only poor but middle-class as well—is shocking.

After decades of pouring money into poor neighborhoods, we know how little good it does. After inner-city Baltimore neighborhoods were ravaged by rioting in 2015, there were calls for "reinvestment" in them. But that's already been done—again and again—and the neighborhoods remain desperate. Development block grants, increases in the minimum wage, and the earned income tax credit may be good ideas, but we need to be realistic. They won't help with the spiritual impoverishment that afflicts the poorest of the poor in America. We cannot buy our way out of Baltimore's moral collapse, a collapse that has spread far into Fishtown. And we need to face the fact that the collapse is encouraged by the nonjudgmental morality favored by Belmont.

A friend of mine worked for a while as a nursing aide—a position at the bottom of the hospital hierarchy, low-paying and often dreary, where his coworkers careened from personal crisis to personal crisis. He once told me, "Yesterday I had to hear the complaints of one woman who was fighting with both her husband *and* her boyfriend." It was the atmosphere of moral disorder that demoralized him, not the menial work.

Teachers can tell similar stories. At a public school in a small midwestern town, an English teacher complains that her students can't understand *The Scarlet Letter* because the act of adultery on which the novel turns seems trivial to them. The drama of concealed sin is lost on kids who live in a world of meth labs, malt liquor, teen pregnancies, and general social collapse.

Today, those who care about the teachings of Jesus must reckon with a singular fact about American poverty: its deepest and most destructive effects, its most serious deprivations, are not economic but moral. Many people below the poverty line have cell phones, flat-screen TVs, and other goodies of our consumer society. In a rich nation like ours, even if you're at the bottom, you still have a lot of stuff. But life is nevertheless impoverished.

How did this come to pass? For the most part we resort to evasions, trying to convince ourselves that the suffering of the poorest among us is primarily economic. More than ten years ago, a graduate student who had grown up in the Soviet Union during its dying decade lived with my family. When a dinner guest, a liberal, expressed concern over the growing divide between rich and poor in America, the Russian scoffed, "There's no poverty in the United States." Our shocked visitor cited a local neighborhood that we all considered utterly blighted. "If you think that's poverty," the Russian replied, "then you've no idea what it's really like to have nothing." How could overweight people living in housing better than the average Soviet apartment building be considered poor? He was right, perhaps, about material poverty, but he had no insight into our society's neglect of the moral, cultural, and spiritual needs of the poor.

The well-to-do often scoff at "family values," but they live by them. They know that family values bring stability, prosperity, and much better chances of a happy, fulfilling life, but they won't say so in public. In fact, they censure those who do, writing us off as the "Religious Right," "culture warriors," and "fundamentalists." Same-sex marriage is the cherry on top of the have-it-all sundae. Edith Windsor, whose lawsuit brought down the Defense of Marriage Act, had an apartment on Fifth Avenue in New York. The case of *United States v. Windsor* concerned taxes on her estate, a liability which affects only those with millions of dollars in assets. Edith Windsor was a One Percenter.

There are other, less glaring ways in which the upper crust has embraced luxury freedoms. Decades ago, the comedian George

Carlin was celebrated for normalizing obscenity. Those at the top end of society could afford a more relaxed attitude. They didn't need to guard their speech as closely as their grandparents had done or exercise strict discipline with their children. Yet among the educated and successful, conversation remains polite. Confrontations, when they occur, don't immediately turn foul. It seems all gain—a less uptight culture that's nevertheless peaceful and polite. But the losses are paid by the poor, whose communities often echo with obscenity and verbal violence.

In New York City rich people routinely deliver a sartorial poke in the eye to those who serve them. The doormen at upscale apartment buildings and the attendants at fancy offices dress formally. It's a sign of respect. But the residents and professionals who live and work there? Tech billionaires and hedge fund moguls come and go in jeans and tee-shirts, thumbing their noses at social expectations, which they can do because they're on top. Dressing like a slob is a way of telling the people who dress up to serve you that they're chumps. This expression of social power—I'm freer from social conventions that you are!—is also common in higher education. The more elite the university, the more likely the professors are to dress down, announcing to the world that they're too powerful and important to worry about social standards.

Today's liberalism is almost entirely focused on cultural politics—abortion rights, sexual liberation, and the strange, twilight battle for sex equality in a society where women outnumber men at universities. These political priorities represent a preferential option for the rich. They favor Belmont residents, who have the

ability to navigate the new freedom, and derail the already struggling people of Fishtown.

Want to help the poor? By all means pay your taxes and give
to charities that provide assistance to those who need it. Volunteer
in a soup kitchen and build a house with Habitat for Humanity.
But you will do more for the poor by resisting nonjudgmentalism.
Exercising the preferential option for the poor means having the
courage to use old-fashioned words such as "chaste" and "honorable," putting on a tie, turning off trashy reality TV shows, and
maintaining standards of deportment. It means restoring a public
culture of moral and social discipline, a discipline Belmont people
need to endorse if they're to exercise cultural leadership for the
sake of the common good rather than their own.

The self-serving and all-powerful ethic of nonjudgmentalism
dictates acquiescence in gay marriage, an exclamation mark on
the trends that have weakened marriage for the poor, and now
"transgender rights," which will further dismantle the develop-
mental norms for children and youth. If we would obey the words
of Jesus, we must resist this pressure. A preferential option for the
poor demands "judgmentalism," which is to say, the courage to
speak forthrightly about right and wrong.

Success Is Not Dignity

Robert Putnam, a Harvard sociologist and self-styled progressive, approaches political matters from a different angle
than Charles Murray, who calls himself a libertarian-leaning

conservative. It's telling, therefore, that Putnam, like Murray, is worried about the fragmentation of America into a well-functioning upper sector and a struggling lower class. In his 2015 book *Our Kids: The American Dream in Crisis* he tells pretty much the same story as *Coming Apart.*

Putnam defines the top and bottom in a straightforward way—the former are college-educated, the latter have a high school diploma or less—providing a rough but useful distinction between today's haves and have-nots. It's Putnam's way of distinguishing between Murray's Belmont and Fishtown, although unlike Murray, Putnam does not focus on white Americans alone.

Putnam's account confirms Murray's. Money? The less educated make less money and are less wealthy. They're more likely to feel financially stressed. Divorce? It's twice as frequent among the less educated. Illegitimacy and single-parent families? Nearly seven times as likely. Rates of imprisonment? Same. Unemployment? Same. Church? The less educated are less likely to attend. Putnam doesn't present statistics on drug use, alcoholism, diabetes, or other dysfunctions, but other sources show that they affect those lower down on the social scale more than those higher up.

In his widely read book *Bowling Alone* (2000), Putnam popularized the notion of "social capital"—the self-discipline, good manners, solid work ethic, and networks of family and friends that prepare one for adult life and constitute a safety net and source of advice, jobs, and advantageous connections. Unlike financial assets, social assets are difficult to quantify.

The sociologist Putnam tries to measure social capital in terms of social trust, breadth of social networks, and even the number of friends people have. You don't need a degree in sociology, however, to anticipate his results. The less educated—Fishtown residents—are more likely to be imprisoned, use drugs, divorce, and have children out of wedlock, behaviors that impede the accumulation of social capital. It's hard to get it together when you're in a community dominated by behavior that tears life apart.

Putnam is less blunt than Murray, but the facts presented in *Our Kids* speak for themselves. The picture is particularly alarming for children. He finds that the children of dysfunctional people have a hard time in life, while the children of functional people have advantages. Putnam's analysis shows that less-educated parents give their children less time and are more likely to neglect and even to abuse them. These kids grow up in run-down neighborhoods with little sense of community. They do poorly in schools that have less rigorous academics and more discipline problems than the schools attended by well-off kids. They're less likely to go to college and far less likely to obtain a four-year or even a two-year degree. They have more difficulty finding steady employment.

Put simply, the children of dysfunctional people tend to be dysfunctional themselves and to pass their dysfunction to the next generation. For those suffering from hereditary dysfunction, the dream of doing better than their parents seems a remote fantasy. A *culture* of poverty is spreading, threatening to turn us into a rigidly two-tiered society. On top are those born to succeed. On the bottom—a growing bottom—are those born to fail. As Murray put it, we're coming apart.

How do we explain this trend toward two Americas? A number of Putnam's critics have chastised him for failing to rally behind the usual progressive answers. Doesn't he see that the poor in America are being hammered by "financial capitalism"? Where is class politics in this book on class? And what about the legacy of racism? Some who agree with my thesis that today's class warfare is moral, not economic, or at least not primarily economic, complain that Putnam doesn't give enough attention to the deregulation of sex and the general pattern of nonjudgmentalism.

Putnam could, of course, say more about capitalism, racism, and the sexual revolution. But within the limitations of *Our Kids*, he strikes the right balance. By my reckoning, the 1950s' wonderfully high wages for men with a high school education were a historical anomaly, attributable to America's unique position as the only intact advanced economy after World War II. Because of our commitment to an open global market, the result in part of the desire to stymie the Soviet Union during the Cold War and to avoid the protectionist policies thought to have contributed to the global crisis in the 1930s, the competitive advantage American workers enjoyed slowly diminished as other nations prospered. At the same time, in the late twentieth century, technological advances shifted work away from manual labor, putting a premium on technical skills that require advanced training.

Conservatives and liberals can argue about the right policy responses to these and other large-scale economic changes, but over the past few decades there has been little debate about embracing globalization and technological innovation. With an economy built on the postwar international system, both Democrats and Republicans consider globalization and innovation necessary for national prosperity, an approach they believe has generally worked to America's advantage. The broad consensus is that since the high-paying manufacturing jobs we enjoyed after the war were unsustainable, the working-class communities built around them were bound to suffer severe strains. This has happened most famously in Detroit but also in Port Clinton, the Ohio town on Lake Erie where Putnam grew up. It's absurd to think the dramatic changes wrought by technology and economic globalization haven't eroded working-class culture. Putnam is right to give them due attention.

Yet it's also absurd to deny that the sexual revolution has exploded the social norms that once brought order and decency to the personal and family lives of working-class people, or that radical feminism hasn't undermined the clear social signals that once steered working-class kids toward productive, sustainable, and complementary roles as men and women. However disorienting it has been for working-class men to compete with low-wage workers in Asia, it's been even more difficult for them—and for working-class women—to make sense out of new social rules that the rich have so quickly adopted and imposed as the new normal.

Putnam details the wreckage with admirable moral sympathy for the victims of the long war on traditional social norms, yet he's reluctant to blame the progressive culture warriors for what their agenda, so popular with the elites, has done to the poor and vulnerable. It's obvious, nevertheless, that most of the liberation projects of the 1960s have been of, by, and for the rich. Betty Friedan, who launched a new and radical wave of feminism in 1963 with *The Feminine Mystique*, was from an upper-middle-class family, went to an elite college, and pursued graduate studies at Cal Berkeley. Prominent gay activists and other proponents of identity politics tend to come from similar backgrounds. Unlike the civil rights movement, led by black men whose social exclusion was almost complete, cultural progressivism has been a top-down project warmly welcomed by establishment institutions.

He might be remiss in assigning responsibility for the dysfunction that plagues the lower class, but Putnam does appeal to the better angels of our nature. Our goal, he says, should be an equal opportunity for everyone to achieve the American dream of a better life than one's parents had. That sounds good, but what counts as a "better" life? Putnam tells us that bad family backgrounds limit "one's ultimate economic success," and that the growing dysfunction in working-class communities undermines "upward socioeconomic mobility." What do the doleful charts of illegitimacy trends and other pathologies tell us? "More single parents means less upward mobility," while "affluent neighborhoods boost academic success." Our biggest problem in America today is an "opportunity gap."

I'm all for upward mobility. It's almost always better to have more and nicer things, and for a democratic culture, a general pattern of upward mobility reassures us that we aren't unjustly limited by our circumstances. We want to believe that individuals can make their own destinies, which is the fuller meaning of the American dream. If enough poor kids get into elite universities or found successful companies—if opportunities seem equal—we think our ideal of limitless opportunity has been vindicated. If *anyone* can succeed, then our society is true to the American dream.

The problem here is Putnam's narrow conception of "success." It's ridiculous to describe the moral and spiritual poverty afflicting the children of today's dysfunctional underclass as a lack of "opportunity." People in Belmont have the luxury of making an idol of success—admission to an elite college, a rewarding career, a well-funded 401(k)—because stable, functional, and usually happy families are taken for granted. More importantly, such families provide the atmosphere of decency and love that are core elements of a dignified life. They're what today's poor have such difficulty attaining.

"Out of the mouth of babes and sucklings," Jesus reminds us, come truths that those in authority fail or refuse to recognize, and *Our Kids*, recording Putnam's numerous interviews with young people, conveys much wisdom, more than the author himself seems to recognize. Andrew, an eighteen-year-old in Bend, Oregon, enjoys every advantage. His father is financially successful. His mom stayed at home during his childhood. He went to a good school. He's off to college with hopes of success there and in his career. But his aspirations, he says, are more basic: "The first thing that would be good for me would be if I could build a home and have a family. Hopefully I will meet somebody that's like my best friend, and then give my kids close to the same as what I had." And what did he receive that he wants to give to his children? "My dad always reminded me every day how much my mom and dad love me." Love—giving and receiving it—is the most precious thing. We desire the freedom that comes from whole-hearted service to what binds our hearts, not freedom for the sake of freedom.

David is roughly the same age as Andrew. His father is in prison; his mother moved out when he was an infant. Both have had revolving-door relationships with alcoholic and drug-addicted partners. His half-brothers and half-sisters are largely neglected, raising themselves. His girlfriend got pregnant recently, but left him after his daughter's birth and now lives with a drug addict. Without skills, a stable family, and a future, David feels he's reached a dead end. In his darkness he does not dream about "success." He's just trying to find his way to the light. He takes care of his neglected siblings when he can and tries to see as much of his daughter as possible. "I love being a dad," he says. He received next to nothing from those who brought him into the world, but David, like Andrew, wants to give. In a disintegrated underclass world that's largely loveless, he too wants to love.

Elijah is a young black man in Atlanta. After a painful and violent childhood, he's a hard, dangerous man who admits, "I just love beating up somebody." Yet Elijah does not come across as a monster. He sees himself with admirable clarity, and he does not like what he sees. He does not love that he loves beating up somebody. "I don't want to go that route now," he tells the interviewer. Instead, he goes to work and to church, "just trying to be a good all-around American citizen." Elijah seeks decency, something more precious than "success."

Putnam's utilitarian, individualistic, and meritocratic assumptions seem to blind him to the basic human aspirations that his subjects voice in these interviews—the desire to give oneself in love, the yearning for decency. He sees institutions like marriage, family, neighborliness, and education as good because they are useful for achieving "success," not as goods in themselves.

Putnam makes much of parents reading to their children, an activity that enhances brain development. The rich are overwhelmingly more likely to do so than the poor, one more advantage the rich give their children in the competition for "success." Yet Andrew cherishes the love shown him by his parents, not their contribution to his brain development. And David longs for a stable family that would allow him to read to his daughter, not to add a couple of points to her IQ, but to bestow on her the gift of his time and attention.

The stories of poor young Americans in *Our Kids* are gut wrenching. They live without stability, without anything resembling a home life, without responsible adults who take care of them—without love. What's missing isn't money. These kids don't want "success." They want decency and a chance to love and be loved.

This unfulfilled longing defines our social crisis. What's wrong with our society today? Why are such simple things so inaccessible to poor people? And why do rich people—even rich people like Robert Putnam, who cares deeply about the poor—seem so blind to the true nature of today's poverty?

Being poor has always been hard, but in the past many of the poor, perhaps most, lived with dignity, even in conditions of serious material want, as Putnam's own stories of Port Clinton in the 1950s reveal. He tells us of his black schoolmate Jesse, whose parents had fled the brutal racial oppression of the South and labored in menial, low-paid jobs. Jesse's parents lacked the opportunity for success as Putnam defines it. Yet only slightly more than a half-century ago, these poor black parents gave their son the steady devotion David longs for, the decent home life Elijah seeks.

Today, self-giving and decency are remote, inaccessible ideals for many poor people in America. Basic human dignity seems out of reach. Raised amid moral chaos, David cannot imagine a functional family in which he could love and care for his daughter. In all likelihood, his own character has been malformed. Even if his circumstances improved, he might lack the self-discipline necessary to follow through on his desire to care for his half-siblings and daughter. David isn't free—not because he lacks money but because he lacks a stable moral environment. The old positional norms that Mary Douglas defended have disintegrated, and nothing has taken their place. He can't do what he most wants to do, which is to live decently and for the sake of others.

I don't want to discount the hardship of material poverty. Being behind on credit card payments, losing your job because your car breaks down and you can't get to work on time, feeling as though the world of opportunity has passed you by—these can be hammer blows on the soul. If rich people are more likely to divorce when a spouse loses a job or piles up debt, the relentless financial battering the poor endure surely contributes to their dysfunction.

We live, moreover, in a consumerist culture that inflames our desire for material things. The poor feel left out when the goodies enjoyed by the middle class and the rich are inaccessible. It's a hypocritical moralist who harrumphs that the poor should be satisfied because they're better off today than the rich were a hundred years ago while he scrambles up the ladder of success, relishing luxuries unimaginable a generation or two ago. That said, we must be clear about our brothers' burdens. Today the poor lack social capital first and foremost, not financial capital. They are spiritually impoverished more than educationally disadvantaged. This poverty is felt in souls, not wallets. Economic and educational reforms may be necessary. We can raise (or lower) taxes, improve our schools, invest in housing, and launch generous social programs, all without making any real difference because moral and spiritual poverty cuts more deeply.

Racism dogged the life of Putnam's black friend Jesse in the 1950s, but the larger culture supported Jesse's parents in their goal of raising their son to be a dignified man: sober, law-abiding, honest, hard-working, faithful to his wife, devoted to his children, and God-fearing. None of these qualities requires "success." None requires the high IQ so prized in today's meritocratic arena. Dignity—the kind the poor kids in Putnam's study so often desire for themselves and those they love, however inarticulately they express it—was once widely accessible. Now it's not.

At least not if you're poor. Putnam, echoing Charles Murray, points out that America has become rigorously segregated. The functional insulate themselves and their children from the dysfunctional. Imbued with a therapeutic ethos that softens the rigors they impose on themselves and their children, and often cowed by multiculturalism, today's rich won't speak up for a common culture that imposes standards on personal behavior. They won't support the traditional common culture that helped Jesse's parents achieve their goal of raising a dignified man. Instead, they quietly and covertly pass on social capital to their children. Their kids go to schools that, for all their celebration of "diversity" and "inclusion," are ruthlessly segregated by social class, ensuring that no "unhealthy" or "anti-social" attitudes infect their charmed world of pleasures without penalties and permissions without punishments. In this controlled, segregated environment, rich kids are prepared for success in today's hypercompetitive meritocracy.

COURAGEOUS JUDGMENTALISM

The preferential option for the poor today means a renewed public commitment to traditional norms about sex, marriage, family, thrift, hard work, and religious faith—in a word, social conservatism. Today's social gospel movement must have the courage to be judgmental.

We can start with policies that punish divorce. I see no reason why we shouldn't have a divorce tax. It could be progressive, applying only to couples who have a net worth of $250,000 (excluding their home). Let's start with a tax of 1 or 2 percent of net worth and increase it to 5 percent for the wealthiest couples. An honest look at working-class America shows that the no-fault divorce revolution has devastated the culture of marriage in poorer communities. The well-to-do who get divorced weaken the institution of marriage, while the social costs of this weakening are largely paid by the poor, who are more vulnerable. Simple justice tells us that the rich should pay to mitigate the damage they inflict on the poor. The tax, which will deter some from getting divorced, can finance programs to remediate, if not reverse, the decline of marriage among the poor.

Those committed to a social gospel should support pro-marriage policies, including educational programs in public schools as well as tax advantages for married couples and other benefits. If we're to counter the destructive trends of family instability, we need to restore a public culture that encourages people to marry and stay married.

There's more to the cultural disintegration devastating the poor than the decline and fragility of marriage. We need to get serious about limiting pornography, a cancer on our society that degrades attitudes toward sex and relationships. Perversely enough, pornographers are treated with great solicitude by judges, while university campuses have become quasi-totalitarian environments with elaborate speech codes.

There's a great deal to be done. I'm not a policy analyst, so I leave it to Christians committed to the poor, and other men and women of good will, to apply themselves to the difficult task of rebuilding a decent public culture that encourages ordinary people to live dignified lives. But let's not kid ourselves—the need is pressing. Since 1960 we have pursued a systematic deregulation of the moral life far more consequential than the financial deregulation liberals decry. And as with economic deregulation, the strong out-compete the weak. As I observed in the last chapter, the powerful today have a monopoly on virtue. They're the nonjudgmental moral experts who know how to "manage difference" and "include" in such a way that an ordinary person is managed, at best, and more often than not excluded as a "bigot."

A free-market proponent can reasonably argue that the economic success of the strong contributes to the common good by increasing GDP, making more resources available to all. We tax economic winners in order to fund programs that redistribute wealth. Moral deregulation, by contrast, serves only the interests of the powerful. We can't tax social capital, nor can we redistribute it.

It's hard to imagine a moral system more conducive to elite domination over ordinary people than nonjudgmentalism, which leaves poor people quite literally demoralized. Increasingly dysfunctional, the poor and near-poor can't form communities and social institutions capable of representing their interests, making it easier for Belmont to dominate Fishtown politically, culturally, and morally. Today's poor and working-class Americans are no longer political subjects with a say in our common future, at least not in the eyes of those who are successful. They are recipients of benefits, patients to be treated, and problems to be managed by their multicultural betters.

The greatest social justice issue of our time is the growing moral inequality of the rich and poor. No invisible hand will correct and guide the moral marketplace. The gay rights project, exemplifying the relentless promotion of lifestyle freedoms that harm the poor, is a sustained assault on a cultural norm of clear rules and patterns for intimate life, the difference between men and women. This assault will continue. The hysterical insistence that the physical reality of male-female differences must be ignored, even denied, for the sake of accommodating transgenderism indicates how limitless this culture war has become.

Without the renewed influence of Christianity, the rich and powerful will not rein in these excesses, which serve their interests. Belmont has shown itself able to adapt quite nicely, while Fishtown disintegrates, making it even easier for the technocratic elite to dominate everything and everyone. Progressives once sought to empower the working class, but today progressivism is an upper-class project. The only hope for the poor comes from those who harken to Isaiah's prophecy of God's anger: "It is you who have devoured the vineyard, the spoil of the poor is in your houses. What do you mean by crushing my people, by grinding the face of the poor?"

CHAPTER 4

PROMOTE SOLIDARITY

T here is a popular assumption, reinforced by propaganda about the Crusades, the Inquisition, and the so-called wars of religion, that religion is a divisive force in society. The reality is otherwise. The socially unifying role of religion in America is empirically well established. Sociological studies show that faith is strongly correlated with social bonding. Religious commitments encourage civic involvement and build social capital. In 2006, a national survey led by Robert Putnam and David Campbell, later published as *American Grace: How Religion Divides and Unites Us*, demonstrated the social benefits of belief in God and regular church attendance. Its unequivocal conclusion was that religious faith makes for better citizens. Religious people are more generous and more involved.

And not just a little more.

Religious people are more likely to volunteer their time—and not just helping out at church. Putnam and Campbell found that slightly more than 40 percent of secular people had volunteered during the previous twelve months, while 60 percent of the most religiously committed had done so. Religious people are more likely than others to volunteer for school and youth programs, neighborhood or civic groups, healthcare organizations, and artistic or cultural programs. "In round numbers, regular church-goers are more than twice as likely to volunteer to help the needy, compared to demographically matched Americans who rarely, if ever, attend church."

Financial generosity also increases—substantially—with reli-giosity. And again, Putnam and Campbell are not simply talking about pious people donating to pious causes. "Regular churchgo-ers are more likely to give to secular causes than nonchurchgoers, and highly religious people give a larger fraction of their income to secular causes than do most secular people."

This generosity isn't surprising. Jesus challenges his followers over and over again in the Gospels. Service to those in need isn't an option. As he warns us, "Truly, I say to you, as you did to the least of these my brethren, you did it to me" (Matthew 25:40). This command to serve others doesn't come with spending caps. We're called to make real sacrifices for the sake of others. By every measure, the more religious you are the more likely you are to vote, attend public meetings, be an officer or a member of a local board, or otherwise take responsibility for your community.

It's also true that religious people are more censorious than nonreligious people, and I submit that this trait, rather than the actual effects of religion on civic life, is the source of faith's bad reputation today. Religious people are judgmental in the sense that they have definite views about right and wrong. The official nonjudgmentalism of our public culture denounces such views as "divisive," a favorite rhetorical sleight of hand that avoids the word "wrong" while still expressing censure. But it turns out that strong moral views, rather than driving people apart, actually build social solidarity. They motivate us to take responsibility. For example, religious people are more likely to consider cheating on one's taxes immoral—by any definition a "judgmental" response—than are those who never or rarely attend church. Moreover, "judgmental" religious people are also the most trusting of others, while the supposedly "nonjudgmental" secularists are less likely to express trust. The promise that multiculturalism and its nonjudgmental ethos will usher in a more harmonious society is simply false.

Religious people's willingness to trust may stem from their humility. Christianity's doctrine of original sin and its consequent pessimism about human behavior paradoxically promote solidarity. We're all sinners, even the best and the brightest, and we need all the help we can get. Nonjudgmentalism, on the other hand, encourages a sense of moral superiority among elites. Political correctness polices rather than trusts.

My progressive friends assume that most southerners are racists, in effect regarding millions of Americans as deeply immoral. In his Supreme Court opinions, Justice Anthony Kennedy decrees that any opposition to the gay-rights agenda can be motivated only by "irrational animus," a charge endlessly echoed in the press. The *New York Times* can spew torrents of invective against social conservatives. And it is religious believers—specifically Christians—who are "judgmental"?

Putnam and Campbell asked people if they agreed with the following statement: "These days people need to look after themselves and not overly worry about others." Nearly half of the secular respondents, 48 percent, agreed, suggesting they are sympathetic to the philosophy of Ayn Rand, the libertarian philosopher of radical individualism. I'm not surprised, because our new meritocracy encourages individualism. Talented young people scramble for places in the top universities, plum internships, and high-paying jobs. Who can afford to worry about others? And anyway, meritocracy encourages us to believe that we've earned our success. If things go badly for others, they're probably getting what they deserve.

This me-oriented attitude shows up in other surveys. Younger liberals are more likely than older liberals to think we've done all we can to address inequality in America. This response may reflect combat fatigue, as it were. The failure to shrink poverty rates can make the "war on poverty" seem futile. But there's also the religious dimension. The younger liberals represent the growing portion of the population with no religious affiliation. Not influenced by a Christian spirit of love, younger liberals gravitate toward freedom's most consistent secular philosophy, libertarianism.

This tilt toward libertarianism, as much a feature of the left as of the right, helps to explain a striking shift in the political priorities of American progressivism. Once focused on working-class and poor Americans, the movement has pivoted to sexual politics. Abortion rights, gay marriage, and now transgender rights are non-negotiable issues for progressives and therefore litmus tests for Democratic politicians. As I argued in the previous two chapters, this shift of political priorities has come at the expense of the weak and vulnerable. An earlier generation of progressives would be perplexed.

A healthy democracy encompasses competing interests and factions. It's unrealistic to expect the powerful to adopt Christ-like self-sacrifice on behalf of the weak and vulnerable, nor should we be seduced by idealistic dreams that ignore the reality of original sin. Nevertheless, a higher degree of solidarity between rich and poor is a reasonable expectation. In the aftermath of World War II, three features of the then all-powerful liberal establishment encouraged its solidarity with the people it governed: patriotic anticommunism, a bourgeois ethic roughly coordinate with the Judeo-Christian moral tradition, and a vague but real connection to religious institutions. Those features have all disappeared. Today's liberal establishment is increasingly internationalist rather than patriotic, nonjudgmental in morality, and decidedly post-religious. In ways unimaginable during the post-war decades, Ivy League graduates and other young elites often unconsciously express a cruel disdain for the social mores of middle America. Many see Walmart as a threat to justice and fast food restaurants as a national blight.

In my youth I was a regular reader of *The New Yorker*, a reliable weathervane of the sentiments of complacent liberalism. In those years the magazine's breezy "Talk of the Town" section taught members of the establishment how to oversee, digest, and otherwise take possession of modern American life with a serene confidence in their superiority. I'm not a regular reader now, and when I picked up an issue a few years ago I was struck by a distinct change of tone. The lead item in "Talk of the Town" focused on a Supreme Court decision upholding the Affordable Care Act. The writer, Jeffrey Toobin, expressed dismay that the court had even heard the case! How dare anyone challenge the Great and the Good! *The New Yorker* is still *The New Yorker*, and Toobin doesn't employ the slashing style of a twenty-first-century blogger, but I was nonetheless surprised. Toobin's political focus and anxious horror seemed alien to *The New Yorker* of my memory, which stood so confidently above the partisan fray. It's a sign of the times: the old establishment that once overarched many social and political differences has evolved into a partisan elite that wages war on those who resist its supereminence.

We Americans have traditionally prided ourselves on our unity. It's part of the very name of our country—the *United* States of America—and proclaimed in our national motto: *e pluribus unum*. But when the governor of New York forbids travel on state business to North Carolina because that sister state's transgender policies are insufficiently enlightened, it's clear that American unity is fraying. Whatever one thinks of the controversial issues roiling our politics, there's a need to bridge the widening social gulf that is making our problems intractable. We need to discover a virtue that our Founding Fathers assumed but never named—solidarity.

THE FALSE PROMISE OF DIVERSITY

Tom and Karen lived on Capitol Hill in Washington, D.C., in the days when it was a neighborhood "in transition," as real estate agents delicately put it—a mix of professional, white newcomers and long-term residents who were mostly poor and black. Tom and Karen liked that mix, the connection with people not like themselves. They joined with their neighbors to improve a common green space on their street. Those neighbors weren't friends, exactly, but they weren't strangers. If you asked Tom and Karen what they liked about their neighborhood, they would have said its "diversity."

Diversity. It's an overused omnibus word that makes me sigh whenever I hear it. The scholar and critic Richard Weaver observed that every society has what he called "god terms"—words or phrases that evoke, often thoughtlessly, what are taken to be its supreme and indisputable goods. In Weaver's day, "democracy" and "progress" were god terms, and along with "freedom" they still have currency. New god terms have emerged since then: "sustainability," for example, and "inclusion." And, of course, "diversity."

Weaver rightly complained that god terms are conversation-stoppers and notoriously vague, but they're unavoidable because we can't explain everything at once. We need summations of our ideals, verbal touchstones, slogans for our ill-defined but heartfelt convictions. Although I can't invoke "diversity" with Tom's and Karen's straight-faced earnestness, I can sympathize with what they want to promote and protect with this god term. The best way to respond to their enthusiasm about the diversity of their neighborhood, then, is to try to understand the ideals, the hopes, the fears, and the suspicions that they pack into that word.

Tom has an advanced degree; Karen went to an elite east coast college. Products of the meritocracy, articulate and self-possessed, they're winners in the game of life as it's now played, with high-power Washington jobs that give them influence and status and more than a decent income. Still, the American democratic spirit, which they share, makes them worry about the temptation to imagine that they're superior and deserve to live on a higher plane than everyone else. This egalitarian conviction has roots in the double heritage of our nation. Christianity teaches that we're all equal in the eyes of God, who is "no respecter of persons," and the Enlightenment insists that all men are endowed with natural rights that are more fundamental than their status in society.

We acknowledge hierarchies. No social system can do without them. On the job the boss is the boss. In the classroom the teacher is in charge. But our Christian and Enlightenment heritage trains us to see these distinctions as necessary in some circumstances but not ultimate. When he has left the parade ground, the private has as much right to be respected as the four-star general. This belief—unique to democratic cultures, rare in human history, and never fully realized—is fundamental.

This commitment to the natural dignity we all share works against a class system in America. Not everybody has the same income or education or status, but we'd like to think that in a deeper sense nobody is above, and nobody below. We want to believe that we all eat the same rations, that our personal destinies are somehow tied to the weal and woe of our fellow citizens.

Walt Whitman, the great poet of the American spirit, wrote of himself, "I encompass worlds and volumes of worlds." That sounds as if he's puffing himself up into some sort of Universal Man. But his meaning is otherwise. Whitman is saying that a true American does not separate himself from his neighbor. He stands neither above nor below him but face to face, sharing a common life and destiny.

That's why Tom and Karen loved Capitol Hill. Walking home from work and greeting their neighbor, a black woman recently retired from the Department of Motor Vehicles, they felt reassured, knowing they shared their lives in many small ways with people less educated, less wealthy, and less privileged. If they didn't quite "encompass worlds and volumes of worlds," they at least enjoyed the neighborliness that keeps our homes from feeling like fortifications against a cold, hostile world.

"Diversity" is a pretty bloodless word for what Tom and Karen loved about their neighborhood. In fact, it's positively misleading. The god term tempts us to think that all we need for a living community of reciprocal obligation is the right demographic recipe. It also tempts us to see others as mere ingredients rather than living persons. We compliment ourselves for having black or Hispanic neighbors, as if their purpose is to make our lives "diverse."

Strictly speaking, diversity is a lifeless statistic. What Tom and Karen cherished but mislabeled is *solidarity*, a condition of sustained personal interaction and reciprocal obligations combined with an internal sense of belonging. Obviously, if we want to promote solidarity with others, we need to make sure they are present, and given our history of racial discrimination, it can make sense to take diversity into account. Unless blacks and whites are present to each other in common activities, institutions, and public spaces, they cannot discern their shared American identity. But often, in a fit of circular reasoning, we promote diversity for the sake of diversity, which gets us nowhere. If taken too far—and it often is—the ideology of diversity works *against* solidarity. Bean-counting to ensure exact representation produces a demographic checklist, not an organic, living community.

Race-based redistricting to guarantee black seats in Congress is a classic example. The predictable result of engineering diversity is Balkanization, with black voters concentrated in a limited number of electoral districts to ensure the election of black representatives. Universities produced the academic version of this phenomenon when they began establishing "black studies" programs in the 1970s, provoking demands for women's studies, gay studies, Native American studies, and on and on. By encouraging students' preoccupation with their ethnic or racial or sexual tribe, these academic set-asides diminish the solidarity that ought to flourish in a university.

When an appropriate attention to diversity is twisted into the ideology of multiculturalism, we are left with no shared culture at all, our common life becoming at best a temporary peace treaty between competing power interests. Multicultural ideology justifies the dominance of elites who are committed to "hearing all voices," "listening to the marginalized," and "promoting diversity." These therapeutic expressions of pseudo-solidarity insulate elites from substantive criticism. Those who challenge them are dismissed as enemies of diversity—racists, bigots, xenophobes.

However misguided in their attachment to the god term diversity, Tom and Karen desire something worthwhile. Solidarity stems from our free assent to unity in the service of a common end. The players on a high school sports team achieve a strong bond through their shared commitment to making the sacrifices necessary to play well and win. Citizens and neighbors committed to sustaining good schools, safe streets, and well-tended parks enjoy a similar bond. National solidarity is not the fruit of diversity. It grows out of common loyalty to our founding principles, identification with our shared history, and the commitment to preserving our heritage for the next generation.

For a religious person, the most perfect expression of solidarity is worship. The church unites around praise of God, our highest end. This unity is not theoretical. Unlike the "international community," which does not exist as a genuine form of solidarity, the Christian community has a genuinely international scope. An evangelical from Dallas can travel to Uganda or China and join in a spiritual communion with his fellow Christians, sharing the Word of God and entering into a fellowship of prayer. The same goes for Catholics, whose church uses the same pattern of liturgical worship throughout the world. When I attend Mass in another country, celebrated in a language I don't understand, I kneel and pray not among strangers but among brothers, with whom I pray to our common Father.

From its beginning, Christianity opposed the use of worship to buttress political unity. Early Christians refused to offer sacrifices to the civic gods of ancient Rome. God transcends the political order. Divine service and the solidarity it engenders are reserved for the city of God, the church, not the city of man. But the Bible endorses national identities as created goods worthy of our loyalty. At Pentecost, the Holy Spirit allows a gathering of people from many different nations to hear the message of Christ in their own languages, not in Esperanto. Our natural forms of solidarity, including nationality, play a role in the divine plan, preparing our hearts for our supernatural union with God and our neighbor. One of the challenges to solidarity today is that post-Christians are often post-patriotic.

PATRIOTISM PROMOTES SOLIDARITY

Rush-hour traffic emerged from the Battery Tunnel and roared up West Street on the gray, overcast afternoon of my first visit to the then newly opened 9/11 Memorial in New York. The site was still surrounded by high fences, and visitors had to pass through metal detectors, which I resented. After the security gauntlet, approaching the open plaza, I felt my heart rate climb and my throat constrict.

The foci of the memorial, designed by Michael Arad, are two square pools sunk deep into the footprints of the fallen towers of the World Trade Center. Thin strands of water cascade down the sides in a delicate screen, collecting in the pools and draining into still deeper shafts at the center that empty into an unseen void. Surrounding the memorial are bronze railings on which are inscribed the names of those who died there on September 11, 2001.

I am looking for the names of three men who were my college classmates. A computerized directory tells me exactly where to find them, and a volunteer asks if I need any help. Uncertain whether I can speak, I croak out, "I've got the names."

Thomas Irwin Glasser, panel S-49. I stand in front of his name and look into the south pool. In my mind I see Tom pitching forward and crumpling into an exhausted heap as he crosses the finish line at a college track meet. I gaze at the plunging water, which evokes the collapsing buildings. The bottomless central drains reinforce the feeling of disintegration. Everything is falling. Everyone is falling.

Douglas Benjamin Gardner, panel N-38, and Calvin Joseph Gooding, immediately to his right, panel N-39. I look again into the falling water and the pitiless drain into which it flows. Images of freshly dug graves flash before my mind. For the briefest moment I see myself hurled down into the abyss of destruction, following the water into the sunken pools and then disappearing into the gaping mouth of the drain. I shudder as I feel the full force of the cold, heartless, annihilating power of death.

Then I turn and look up at One World Trade Center, the massive building we're no longer supposed to call the Freedom Tower—to avoid jingoism, I suppose. Apparently, the workmen haven't gotten that memo, for draped on the side of the building is the largest American flag I've ever seen. My emotions shift. In my imagination I'm hearing bugles rallying the troops, and Tom and Doug and Calvin rise together to answer. My soul, disintegrated by death's dark power, hardens with resolve. I feel a consolation that neither cancels nor denies nor forgets their deaths, but fuses my private sense of loss to something larger, durable, and noble. A living, particular American "Yes" overwhelms death's universal "No."

The giant flag on One World Trade Center was not part of the 9/11 Memorial plan, and it's not there anymore. Arad called his design "Reflecting Absence." In its death-focused nihilism, the memorial allows room only for private grief, not our capacity to transcend death in our public loyalties. Ever the soulless technocrat, Mayor Michael Bloomberg reinforced this exclusion by sidelining patriotic symbols and gestures at the ceremony marking the tenth anniversary of the attacks. But the Freedom Tower is owned by the Port Authority of New York and New Jersey, not the City of New York. The day before the ceremony, and just a few days before my visit, in what it called a "spur-of-the-moment decision," the Port Authority hung the enormous flag on the side of the building that faces the 9/11 Memorial.

It was a welcome act of resistance to the post-patriotic mentality. The absence of religious symbolism in the memorial is an acknowledgment of America's, and especially New York City's, pluralism, but the memorial also rejects national symbolism. There are no flags, no eagles, no emblems of American identity. There are only the names on the bronze rails surrounding the falling water, a note of private, individual remembrance of loss that is somehow false. Osama bin Laden did not target my friends. He targeted our country.

The emphasis on the personal comes as no surprise. A prominent member of the 9/11 Memorial committee was Maya Lin, whose acclaimed Vietnam Veterans Memorial in Washington, with the names of those who died in Southeast Asia inscribed on its long black wall, reflects a similar approach.

What succeeds in Washington fails in New York. National symbolism is everywhere in Washington, so Lin's reticence works against a background of clear and forceful patriotism. Downtown Manhattan is dedicated to global commerce, not American patriotism. The tall buildings clad in featureless glass surrounding the 9/11 Memorial look exactly like tall buildings in Shanghai and Dubai. Global capitalism tells us we are not Americans (or Chinese or Nigerians); we are managers and workers, producers and consumers. The faceless, placeless, symbol-shorn architectural vocabulary of the 9/11 site tells us we are naked and homeless in the global system that produces vast wealth but no public meaning. We're alone in the great scramble for wealth, alone in our grief over the ruthless power of death.

This atomized condition, stripped of public meaning, leaves us vulnerable to tyranny. In a world with no common commitments, ordinary people have no place to stand and resist the powerful. To be frank, this atomizing, disempowering effect served the interests of today's technocratic elite, which is why they prefer a symbol-shorn, modernist architectural style. They like the way it forms post-religious, post-patriotic individuals defined solely by the pursuit of private self-interest. Atomized, self-interested people are more easily managed than those united in a common purpose. They are easier to dominate than those willing and able to make sacrifices for the sake of a transcendent loyalty.

In ancient Greek *pater* means "father," *patria* means "ancestry," and *patris* means "place of one's ancestors." Latin takes on this meaning without alteration. *Patria* means "fatherland," and *patriota* means "countryman." These are words signifying deep attachments, continuities, and duties. A patriot loves his place of birth; he rises to defend it when it is threatened. Patriotism, a habit of devotion or piety, encourages loyalty, disposing us to be selfless in service to the nation, willing to sacrifice our self-interest for the sake of our shared inheritance.

Mid-twentieth-century totalitarianism perverted patriotism, absorbing the individual into a supposedly higher and sacred collective destiny: the dictatorship of the proletariat, the thousand-year

Reich, and so forth. But this is not the only way to destroy freedom. Our present-day elites now tend to work in the opposite direction, not constructing false schemes of transcendence but denying the possibility of transcendence and thus dissolving our higher loyalties. Like the nonjudgmentalism that dismantles the moral architecture of working-class life, exaggerated warnings about the dangers of nationalism and ethnocentrism isolate and atomize us. The 9/11 Memorial is part of a larger trend that seeks to repress patriotism.

Nationalism and ethnocentrism can distort and betray the true spirit of patriotism and other forms of solidarity. We need to be vigilant in our loves, purifying them through appropriate criticism and examination. Yet this is not what is being sold to us today. In the place of a purified solidarity, one that reminds us of what is truly worthy of loyalty and sacrifice, elites offer therapeutic experiences. We see this tendency in the way our leaders now talk about 9/11. They focus on "tragedy," "loss," and "healing." The 9/11 Memorial is almost entirely organized around this therapeutic approach, which tries to create a "sensitive" atmosphere for us to "explore" our own "meanings."

In his enthusiastic review of the 9/11 Memorial, Martin Filler expressed dismay at the reactions of some family members of the victims. One complained, "There should have been flowers or pictures or something." That's a natural impulse. Faced with death and alone in our grief, we want to express our emotions and honor the dead against the background of something *alive*—a simple, shared tradition of memorial flowers, perhaps, or religious ritual, or a reminder of the larger national narrative in which 9/11 plays a part.

Filler's response is telling: "But of course it is precisely the abstract nature of Arad's design, which eschews all representational imagery, that allows visitors to project onto it thoughts and interpretations of a much more individual nature than if the memorial had been laden with pre-packaged symbols of grief." The same dismissive response would apply, I suppose, to my own desire for flags. Filler represents the elite mentality that Mary Douglas saw at work in the attack on traditional Catholic rituals like Friday abstinence. People like me are afraid of real freedom—the freedom to make our own meanings for ourselves.

This is sold to us as empowerment. I can imagine a memorial volunteer trained by Filler saying, "We cannot pretend to tell you, dear visitor, what 9/11 means for you. We can only facilitate your personal journey." But a reduction to individual meaning is not empowering. The therapeutic approach reflects what Pope Benedict XVI famously called "the dictatorship of relativism," a regime of opinion that dissolves strong convictions. The great achievement of the democratic era was to transform passive subjects into active citizens, but by repressing national symbols, the dictatorship of relativism isolates us from each other. Without strong public symbols of unity—without *solidarity*—we return to the role of passive subjects. Denied public identities and encouraged to think and act in a world of self-chosen meanings, we remain alone in our private world. Because there is no shared public realm infused with public meaning, we can't challenge the powerful in public.

As national symbols are repressed ("We don't want jingoism!") and forthright moral language set aside ("We mustn't be judgmental!"), the role of leaders changes. Patriotism encourages a sense of common purpose, as do shared moral convictions, which assure that all men are judged by the same moral law. In the dictatorship of relativism, you and I are managed therapeutically by experts rather than engaged as fellow citizens. In a moment of candid condescension, Barack Obama dismissed his small-town opponents as embittered simpletons who "cling to guns or religion or antipathy to people who aren't like them," implying that dissent is a condition to be diagnosed and managed rather than a rational argument to be engaged and answered. Even when today's elite try to engage ordinary people, they speak therapeutically of "empowerment"—something the powerful condescend to do *for* us rather than what we do together.

I am not entirely pessimistic. On the day I visited the 9/11 Memorial, somebody left a small American flag wedged in the top of the "P" of James Patrick Leahy's name. Like the patriotic sentiment it expressed, the small wooden shaft fit perfectly. The solitary little flag, like the giant one hanging from the Freedom Tower, expressed a patriotic emotion integral to a free society. Ordinary people are extraordinary when united in the service of something higher. We need patriotic solidarity to hold the powerful accountable—and to unite against them when they go astray.

The danger here is that patriotism, like all strong loyalties, can be distorted. A renewal of patriotism needs to be linked, therefore, to a renewed faith, for the love of God transcends all earthly loves. The Gospel of Jesus Christ is infinitely more precious than the American way of life.

There is something comical about an ardent nationalist. He champions his homeland with little sense of her failings or the achievements of other nations and cultures. Such a man is in love with the idea of his country, not with its living reality. America has had her share of puerile patriots. Perhaps I too have been seduced by a nationalistic pride, which sees being "number one" as the be-all and end-all of a nation's existence. This is boosterism, not patriotism. As G. K. Chesterton observed, the real meaning of "my country right or wrong" is "my mother drunk or sober." Our loyalty is to her, not to her sobriety, and is entirely consistent with criticizing her drunkenness.

So yes, let's beware of American boosterism. But let's also avoid a hypercritical mentality that cannot rouse itself to the warmth of patriotic feeling. The failings of our country no more merit the forfeiture of our love than do the failures of our parents. If anything, the defects in our national character call for love's greater measures of devotion. When Martin Luther King, Jr. invoked the Declaration of Independence's assertion of the self-evident truth of equality, when he recited the rousing first stanza of the "Battle Hymn of the Republic," he was not cynically shaping his "message" to appeal to white listeners. He was appealing to our common love, calling us to a national conversion for the sake of our country's highest ideals.

We need to strengthen patriotic loyalties today, not weaken them. As the pressures of globalization divide our country into economic winners and losers, the top 20 percent—Charles Murray's Belmont—will be tempted to transfer its loyalty from America to the global economy and the network of organizations that have risen to serve it. The consulting firm McKinsey is no longer an "American" company, at least not in the way it once was. Silicon Valley presses for relaxed immigration laws so that it can hire talented engineers and scientists in a global marketplace. The wealth-producing machine is now global. Enhancing and protecting and profiting from that machine increasingly preoccupies upper-crust Americans, redefining their loyalties.

Elite universities show how the top end of society is drawn toward a post-American outlook. Many have opened campuses in the Middle East and Asia, motivated in part by the desire to bank as much foreign cash as possible. But there's also a self-conscious desire to redefine their roles as global rather than national. They want to train the world's elite, not just America's. At the same time as financiers and tech entrepreneurs are more dependent on a global system that allows them to invest, hire, and market without regard to national interest, the culture-transmitting institutions in America are edging away from what was once a self-consciously national and patriotic purpose.

This shift away from patriotism is masked by Americans' sense that, since our country dominates the world, to be an American citizen is to be a global citizen. But we should not be deceived. As we continue "coming apart," the most powerful and successful Americans increasingly see that their interests lie with a global future, not a national one. A Fortune 500 CEO has more in common with other Davos worthies than with the son of an unemployed steel worker in Youngstown, Ohio. Educated at institutions steeped in multicultural ideology, the elite rise above local loyalties, serving as richly rewarded functionaries in a global empire that has no place for patriotism because it has no *patria*.

Nonetheless, the overwhelming majority of Americans remain viscerally patriotic, and patriotism encourages us to serve the common good, even to the point of sacrificing our lives. It is patriotism that motivates us to stick with each other, even when we're coming apart. Patriotism restores solidarity.

RENEWING SOLIDARITY

Friedrich Hayek wrote his classic *The Road to Serfdom* during World War II in the hope of shaping the postwar reconstruction of society. The West, he believed, faced a decisive choice: to affirm individual freedom or to embrace central planning and socialism. Today, however, our greatest threat is untethered individualism. We're living in a dissolving society, not a collectivist one.

In the most widely read book by a progressive economist in recent years, *Capital in the Twenty-First Century*, Thomas Piketty argues that capitalism breeds substantial and growing inequalities. Instead of following up this analysis with a call for socialism or some other collectivist utopia, however, he suggests policies that will *save* capitalism from its own excesses. You can disagree with every sentence in *Capital in the Twenty-First Century*, but there's no disputing that it's representative of our times. Before the fall of the Soviet Union, we thought we could choose between capitalism and socialism, but that historical moment has passed. Today, progressives are capitalists too.

It's a mistake to think we face a socialist, collectivist threat. In America, where a pro-capitalist consensus encompasses both parties, the debate about taxes operates within a narrow range. Are we going to ding top earners at 35 percent or 39 percent? This is hardly a culture-defining question of the sort that concerned Hayek. Labor unions exercise less and less influence in our economy. Largely confined to public employees, they are really political action committees angling to capture tax revenue rather than a large-scale movement contesting with owners of capital for economic power.

Global capitalism, far from being hobbled by excessive regulation, unionization, and taxation, has gone from strength to strength over the past few decades, transforming societies throughout the world, especially in Asia. While a free market encourages initiative, innovation, and growth, it also brings creative destruction. From 1950 to 1970, the average earnings of American male workers increased by 25 percent each decade, but since then, men earning the median wage have seen no growth in earnings, even though

GDP has doubled since 1975. And as we have seen, the cultural foundations of middle-class life have eroded over the same period.

It is the economic and cultural dissolution of the American middle class that defines our moment in history, not squabbles over tax policy, regulation, and green energy subsidies. There is a growing feeling that the American social contract has been revised. Identity politics spring from the dissolution of the middle class. It's the Democratic Party's strategy to find a new basis for a securing governing majority, a rainbow coalition of grievances that will replace the old middle class consensus.

When American conservatives speak of economic freedom today, they can sound irrelevant, even perverse. The free flow of capital, goods, services, and labor is all well and good if you're one of the winners in the global economy. But what's in it for the high-school-educated guy in Toledo who has to compete with low-wage workers in Thailand? If the Democratic Party's enthusiasm for global capitalism is muted, its enthusiasm for lifestyle freedom is at full volume. Its commitment to moral deregulation, even if it dissolves the middle class, is absolute.

What does Hayek have to say to such a world? Individual freedom was his great emphasis. In *The Road to Serfdom*, he sounds a libertarian note, arguing that "individuals should be allowed, within defined limits, to follow their own values and preferences rather than someone else's; that within these spheres the individual's system of ends should be supreme and not subject to any dictation by others." In the context of 1940s European totalitarianism,

the sentiment was admirable. But today an approach that emphasizes individualism may do more harm than good.

I don't have answers to the challenges posed by the dissolution
of middle-class America, an epoch-defining change in our society.
I incline toward free markets and am suspicious of large-scale
government interventions. But the weakening middle class poses
the most profound challenge to America today. Freedom can be
threatened by centralized planning, but it is also diminished when
we have no solid ground on which to stand. Today, many Americans are standing on increasingly unstable economic and cultural
ground, and they're less and less free.

We hope that greater economic opportunity is the path to
prosperity and solidarity. Robert Putnam's *Our Kids* was well
received because it focuses on expanding opportunity. Many
want to believe that this will repair our frayed social contract,
because the notion that more people can "make it" fits with our
dream of freedom and its emphasis on individual initiative. But
it won't work. Expanded opportunity fails to address our deeper
problem, which is the demise of a once powerful and unifying
consensus. Even if a few more kids from Fishtown make it to law
school, we'll still have two Americas, a divided country in which
we have less confidence that all of us are playing by the same
rules, sharing the same burdens, and enjoying the same benefits.

We're facing a crisis of solidarity, not freedom, and this crisis
of solidarity foretells a crisis of freedom. Atomized, isolated individuals adrift in a deregulated moral culture are easily dominated,

whether by political manipulators or the directionless leadership of mass culture.

A Christian society recognizes the importance of solidarity. Christians know we serve neither history nor destiny nor progress. We are not drawn together by GDP. An ever-greater utility, fevered dreams of sexual freedom, and equality of the sexes are devouring abstractions, not bases for solidarity. A frictionless free market may promote economic growth, but it cannot bind us together in a living community. A nation is more than a scaled-up limited liability corporation. As our shared civil life is diminished, a Christian seeks the common good. He criticizes America, but with a spirit of loyalty, resisting the post-patriotic mentality. We mustn't seek the social weightlessness that liberates the rich and powerful while atomizing and disempowering most citizens. To love our neighbor we need to love our neighborhood.

CHAPTER 5

LIMIT GOVERNMENT

W e need to limit government to fend off tyranny. A benevolent king with unlimited power might seek the good of his people, and some have. His subjects might enjoy freedom of speech, association, and religion. He might smile on a vigorous press, even indulge it when it had the temerity to criticize him. But it would be political foolishness to rely on the good will of the powerful. We cannot count on virtue in high office, especially not when it puts great power in the hands of fallen men.

Democracy, the Founders recognized, poses a parallel danger. A democratic majority is no more to be trusted with our freedom than a solitary sovereign. In the modern ideology of democracy, the majority rules not just as a matter of procedure but by moral right, claiming an absolute authority that would make Louis XIV blush. Divine-right monarchy at least acknowledged—in theory, anyway—the higher authority of God. Modern theories of democracy rarely acknowledge a transcendent limit on the power of the people.

The evolution of democracy into tyranny is a familiar theme in modern history. The French Revolution produced the Terror and then Napoleon's dictatorship. The Weimar Republic limped along for a dozen years, only to dissolve when the people's elected representatives gave Hitler supreme power, a decision soon ratified by an overwhelming popular vote.

With this danger in mind, the framers of the U.S. Constitution designed a system of checks and balances to limit the power of the federal government. The separation of the judicial, legislative, and executive powers prevents their accumulation in a single arm of government. A representative system divided between the House of Representatives and the Senate blocks direct democratic rule. The first ten amendments, the Bill of Rights, imposed particular limits on government power.

In view of the tremendous growth of the United States in population, wealth, and power over the past two centuries, the American constitutional regime has proved remarkably durable. Nevertheless, the Civil War, which definitively established the supremacy of the national power over individual states; the Great Depression, World War II, and the Cold War, which provoked the mass mobilization of society, enlarging the federal government and expanding its powers; and the civil rights legislation of the mid-1960s, which extended federal oversight to every corner of society, produced a vast and superordinate federal apparatus that the Founders would scarcely recognize.

Nor have the Bill of Rights and later amendments designed to protect freedom always been effective checks on the power of government. In spite of these constitutional guarantees, courts have countenanced the government takeover of the Mormon church in the nineteenth century, legally enforced racial segregation, various waves of drastic anticommunist efforts, and the internment of Japanese-American citizens during World War II. The majority gets its way more often than not.

We would be wrong to conclude that the American Constitution has failed, for only a foolishly legalistic mind imagines that a healthy culture of freedom can be created by laws. We can do our best to formulate laws and design institutions that will protect liberty by limiting government power, but politics can do only so much. The Founders designed a constitution with checks and balances, but more important still are the checks and balances provided by culture. Over the long run, only the countervailing power of a healthy culture—itself the product of a healthy religion—can keep the power of the state in check.

Subsidiarity

The Founders expected the states—each a distinctive society commanding the loyalty of its people—to play a decisive role in limiting the power of the federal government. The upper house of Congress, for example, is essentially a forum of the states, each state legislature selecting two senators without respect to the state's size. (The Seventeenth Amendment in 1913 changed the system, requiring senators to be elected by state-wide popular vote.) The federal government possesses only those powers specifically enumerated in the Constitution, the states retaining the primordial sovereign power to legislate for the safety, health, morals, convenience, and general prosperity of the public.

This constitutional structure, known as federalism, reflects the Founders' intuition that power is most beneficially exercised at the lowest level practicable, a principle that the Catholic Church would elaborate on in the body of social teaching that emerged in the twentieth century. In 1931, on the fortieth anniversary of Leo XIII's *Rerum novarum*, Pope Pius XI issued the encyclical letter *Quadragesimo anno*, written for an epoch of mass production, mass entertainment, and mass mobilization of armies. Addressing the tendency of large corporations and even larger governments to absorb all of life into their economic, bureaucratic, and nationalist projects, the pope formally articulated the principle of subsidiarity, according to which "it is an injustice and at the same time a grave evil and disturbance of right order to assign to a greater and higher association what lesser and subordinate organizations can do."

Pius XI identified a basic need for *breathing room*. We don't want every aspect of our lives to be regulated from above by distant bureaucrats or dominated by multinational corporations.

Subsidiarity, the principle that ensures breathing room, takes its name from the Latin *subsidium*, which means "aid" or "assistance," but it's also related to *sub sedeo*, "I sit underneath." The greater powers in modern society, especially the state, should assist the institutions that "sit underneath" them, helping them flourish and exercise a real role in the ordering of society. These great powers must never "destroy and absorb" them.

The "lesser and subordinate organizations" that Pius XI defended are what social theorists call "mediating institutions"— non-governmental bodies such as labor unions, the Boy Scouts, PTAs, Rotary Clubs, softball leagues, and neighborhood associations, as well as churches and other religious institutions. Bringing citizens together to solve local problems on their own, or to influence government agencies or large corporations in appropriate ways, mediating institutions provide the small-scale opportunities for solidarity that are essential for a free society. The dramatic success of the civil rights movement, for example, would be unimaginable without the spiritual nourishment and organizational work of the black churches.

The modern welfare state, absorbing one social function after another, has become a grave threat to mediating institutions. It tends to crowd out or co-opt them. Federal education grants are increasingly conditioned on compliance with any number of social policies, eroding the autonomy of local school boards. Federal healthcare funding likewise has greatly diminished the autonomy of private hospitals, including those operated by religious institutions. With the push for universal preschool, the state is assuming even the most basic role of the family, the care of small children.

In the face of this trend, respect for subsidiarity requires that the largest, most powerful institutions in society, especially the state, not overwhelm smaller institutions, which may mean accepting their imperfections. Where locally governed and funded public school systems produce uneven results, progressives—often blind to the intrinsic good of small-scale, self-governing units of society—see a problem to solve, usually through state-wide or even national "standards" and funding. The goal of educational reform should be more than improved test scores; reform should preserve an American tradition of local responsibility.

It's not enough to avoid interfering in mediating institutions, however. Subsidiarity entails nurturing and empowering them. The dramatic decline in social involvement among the poor that Charles Murray identifies in *Coming Apart* reflects the decline of mediating institutions in their neighborhoods. Fishtown residents have few bonds uniting them and few places where they can unite to solve local problems. The principle of subsidiarity encourages government to provide assistance to whatever institutions remain, including *religious* institutions.

It is frequently argued that a local church or community organization understands local needs and problems better than distant bureaucrats do and is therefore able to address them more effectively and at less expense. That may well be true, but subsidiarity is not primarily about efficiency. We should encourage the development of local institutions for their own sakes. It is good for ordinary people to be involved in sustaining and improving their communities.

Explaining why requires going back to Aristotle.

Defining man as a rational animal, Aristotle concluded that his happiness is to be found in the fullest use of his reason, that is, in the contemplation of truth. But Aristotle recognized that most people aren't reflective, at least not spontaneously so. Most of us are preoccupied with health, wealth, and wellbeing. Even these mundane concerns, however, can lead to a noble, elevating exercise of reason when, coming together to organize our common life, we identify the common goods we share and how to achieve them, as well as defining the just order of society. Such public deliberation is the essence of politics, which Aristotle sometimes called the highest good for man. (At other times he is something of a philosophical purist and designates contemplation as the highest good.)

Aristotle thought only free Athenian males were up to the task of using their reason in this way. The principle of subsidiarity takes a more optimistic and democratic view. It's not that everyone is involved in politics in the narrow modern sense of the affairs of state. In fact, universal involvement in the affairs of state would be contrary to the principle of subsidiarity. Mediating institutions are themselves "political" in the broad sense of being self-governing civic organizations, and they can have more influence on our daily lives than what's happening at the state capital or in Washington.

The principle of subsidiarity thus promotes man's political vocation. That does not mean running for office, which few are suited for, or voting, a momentary political act remote from the actual exercise of political power. Involvement in mediating institutions draws us into long-term responsibilities for living social organisms—a book club, a neighborhood association, a school, a choral society. Subsidiarity promotes human dignity because it encourages a thick local culture that encourages our free, responsible participation.

America is undergoing deep and wrenching changes, the economic side of which is usually discussed in terms of income inequality. Far less notice has been given to the equally important crisis in subsidiarity and the resulting civic inequality. Progressives think that troubled cities like Baltimore suffer from too little investment in social programs and urban redevelopment. But poor neighborhoods in Baltimore are dysfunctional *because there are no functional local institutions*. Even the churches, once the backbone of poor black communities, are weakened. The institutions with which the poor interact are almost entirely governmental—public schools, health and welfare agencies, and, of course, the police, the courts, and the prison system.

The crisis of subsidiarity affects more than poor blacks. Half a century ago it was easy to picture a dockworker in Baltimore who was married, a union member, living in an ethnic neighborhood, participating in his parish, and drinking with childhood pals at the Sons of Italy hall. That same working-class guy today? Even if he has a job, his level of social engagement is much lower, in part because mediating institutions are weaker, civic culture thinner, and expectations for what it means to be a grownup lower.

We have become depoliticized, not in the narrow sense of losing interest in elections (though that can be a symptom) but in the more important sense of no longer participating in the intimate, local self-governing institutions that depend on us for their success. Without responsibility for sustaining those institutions, without the discipline of self-government, we focus on ourselves, falling into consumerism and hedonism. Video games have become our national pastime.

Into these depoliticized communities creeps the ever-expanding bureaucratic-therapeutic state with its promises to take care of us. As mediating institutions weaken and disappear, we become more docile to the ministration of our betters. The Bill of Rights still protects us. The constitutional separation of powers remains. But as our capacity for self-governance declines, we lose our sense of what it means to be free.

"We." That's not entirely right. As Charles Murray reports, rich Americans are involved in local organizations. In Belmont, with its wide array of mediating institutions, volunteerism flourishes. There are bake sales and fund raisers. Parents are perfectly capable of mounting resistance to state educational policies they think unsuitable for their kids. Among the rich, self-government is strong.

The result is a political culture organized around Belmont's concerns. The Democrats, traditionally the party of labor unions, have become the party of the top 20 percent—specifically, those successful people who prefer expert, technocratic management of society. The Republicans may get votes from religious and social conservatives, but they too have become the party of the top 20 percent—specifically, those who like free markets. The other 80 percent has become politically inert. If they're over forty, they're manipulated by thirty-second TV spots; if they're under forty, by social media. This political culture features mock-democratic struggles among the meritocratic elite, those on the left supporting abortion rights and gay marriage, those on the right supporting tax cuts. The terms of the debate are set entirely by the elites, until a populist politician comes onto the scene to disrupt this top-down political culture. But without a capacity for self-government encouraged by participation in local affairs, even the most potent eruptions of populism are likely to fizzle.

Can we revive mediating institutions for ordinary people? Immigration, economic mobility, and the advent of mass culture in the early twentieth century; the common, unifying experience of a global war; and other profound cultural changes have so weakened the local loyalties the Founders took for granted that Robert E. Lee's anguished decision not to draw his sword against Virginia is now incomprehensible to the average twenty-five-year-old. In a country of individuals unattached to a particular family and a particular way of life in a particular place, the power of government flows unimpeded into every nook and cranny once occupied by subsidiary institutions.

I'm not optimistic about mediating institutions. Belmont will maintain strong local organizations and a capacity for self-governance, but most Americans live in a more fluid, individualistic environment. So we must go deeper—and higher. If we hope to limit government, we must renew the two institutions that antedate it—marriage and religion. Although they too have been weakened, the intimate society of the family and the sacred society of the faithful remain powerful social forces. Properly understood and encouraged, they can keep government in its place, marriage acting from below, religion from above.

LIMITING FROM BELOW

The family is the most ancient and enduring of what Edmund Burke called the "little platoons." Our primary loyalty, encouraged by nature, is to our parents, brothers and sisters, spouse, and children. If properly cultivated and purified of an insular, tribal tendency, the capacity to give ourselves in love to our relatives can grow into a love of community and country and the still greater love of God.

Forms of family life have changed over the centuries. While it once extended to the clan, today it is more nuclear—husband, wife, and kids. Whatever its form, the family is an integrated, independent social unit that thoroughly shapes us. Most of us understand intuitively what social science has demonstrated repeatedly: the most decisive influences on children come from within the family.

The family is society in miniature, our first and most enduring experience of political life. In the family we learn the meaning of the common good, in this case the good of the family unit. It is more than the sum of satisfied individual desires. We feel the tug of solidarity and subordinate our self-interest to the service of the whole. In the family we learn the meaning of legitimate authority. Parental authority seeks the good of children, serving as a model for public authority exercised for the sake of those ruled rather than of the rulers.

The true meaning of peace becomes clear to us in family life as well. Sexual intercourse may produce children, but it does not form a family. Only an ongoing partnership, bridging the male-female divide, does that. In this partnership, which we call marriage, a man and a woman become a single social unit. Transcending their individual projects, needs, and desires, they live in unity instead of division, in peace instead of conflict.

Marriage is so common, so familiar that we forget that a permanent, harmonious male-female union is quite improbable. A social worker I know once shared the youthful, egalitarian conviction that men and women are the same. Working with poor black women cured her of that delusion. The differences between men and women—their self-images, motivations, social instincts, and goals—were at the center of most of the problems she was trying to help them deal with. "You can't live with 'em," one of her clients said, repeating a timeless lament about the opposite sex, "but you can't live without 'em." There's a perennial war between the sexes, and my friend gradually realized that, if unchecked, this war makes life miserable. Most of the women she helps take refuge in a sisterhood of sorts. But that's only a partial solution, because they aren't able to give up on men.

Some societies allow polygamy, others arranged marriages. The conditions for the dissolution of marriage vary. In Western Europe, the official institution of marriage has declined, but a practice of unofficial marriage has emerged in its place. A child born in France is more likely to grow up with his natural parents than one born in the United States even though men and women are much less likely to marry in France. But for all this variety, there is one constant across every culture: marriage resolves the primal feud between men and women.

That's certainly the biblical message. At the heart of St. Paul's letter to the Ephesians is his charge to the Christian community to live "with patience, forbearing one another in love, eager to maintain the unity of the Spirit in the bond of peace" (4:2). Addressing husbands and wives in particular, the apostle invokes the promise from Genesis that in marriage "the two shall become one" and calls the nuptial bond a "great mystery." Signifying the union between Christ and the Church, the peace-making role of marriage points to the good news that Christ's sacrifice on the cross has healed the breach between sinful humanity and God's eternal righteousness, uniting us with him in peace.

We shouldn't underestimate the political importance of marriage as a peace-making institution. It is in the family that a child receives his formative experiences of political life in a fallen world. If his parents achieve a workable harmony, he learns how solidarity— unity in spite of profound differences—serves a common good, and he is more likely to understand society as a permanent bond between citizens, not a temporary aggregation of self-interested individuals.

Political philosophers have always regarded marriage and the family as a force to be reckoned with. Plato speculated that the ideal city must destroy its influence in order to form young people in accord with a purely philosophical view of the good life. The seventeenth-century monarchist Sir Robert Filmer saw paternal authority as the paradigm for all forms of political authority. The liberal John Locke, by contrast, downplayed the family, stipulating that the authority of parents ended when their children reached the age of majority. Society, in other words, is not the family "scaled up." Locke's ideal society is instead a free association of individuals, unbound by duties that transcend their choices. Modern revolutionaries don't ascribe to Lock's liberalism, but they too have been wary of the family, even hostile. Moderate progressives, like more ardent ones, are intent on government control of education. Social change requires overriding the authority of parents over children so that the authority of reason (or history or progress) can prevail.

We don't have to sort through these different views of the family and politics to see that they all recognize the political importance of the family, for good or ill. We regard what goes on in our homes as "private" not because it is inconsequential for public life but because we jealously guard family life from government intrusion. Citizens who feel competent to run their households, manage family finances, and raise children will fight back when government tries to run their lives.

Decades ago, the field we now call "family law" was pretty much confined to registering marriages and births, arbitrating the occasional divorce, and ratifying adoptions. That's changed. As poor and working-class households have sunk into dysfunction, government has assumed responsibility for much of their domestic affairs. Three generations ago, there was little government support for families, but today the earned income tax credit and food stamps are indispensable financial props for millions of families. There are pre-kindergarten programs and free meals at school, while social workers try to help single mothers balance work and childcare. Churches and other charities do their best to help children growing up without fathers.

All this assistance is well intentioned, often necessary. In a society without clear sex roles, without taboos against cohabitation, illegitimacy, and divorce—which is to say, without powerful social norms governing individual behavior—governmental and quasi-governmental support (and therefore control) necessarily expand. The triumph of nonjudgmentalism has created a cultural vacuum. The void is now filled by laws, lawyers, and courts that adjudicate the conflicts that arise in the private lives of ordinary people. Moral deregulation brings a certain kind of freedom, but someone has to pick up the pieces. More often than not, that "someone" is the government, or someone acting at the behest of the government, financed by a government grant.

Recently the Supreme Court pushed us past another milestone when it redefined marriage. From time immemorial, nations have recognized the institution of marriage, legally regulating the union of man and wife. Divorce too—though relatively rare until the 1960s—existed in one form or another as far back as biblical times. The no-fault divorce laws that became the norm fifty years ago, however ill-considered, were not inventions of lawyers and activists. The cultures and laws of the nations of the world embodied varying standards with respect to polygamy, the age of consent, consummation, and marital property. There has always been a great deal of diversity in the details of marriage custom and law. But legislators, judges, and kings have always regarded the marital union of man and woman as a given, a prepolitical institution to be recognized and regulated, not redefined.

In its revolutionary decision in *Obergefell v. Hodges*, the Supreme Court broke with this tradition, treating marriage as a plastic social form to be reconfigured at will. There is not the slightest suggestion in the Bible, the common law, or the Constitution that a man can marry a man or a woman can marry a woman. The court simply took possession of marriage, treating it as a purely government-defined institution. The meaning of marriage is now entirely in the hands of the political process. Whoever controls the government controls marriage. It means whatever five judges—or a majority of voters—decide.

If government can redefine marriage, it can redefine everything else in private life. What does it mean for a child to have parents? There's no reason to think the political process will yield to nature. For decades, laws have bestowed anonymity on sperm donors, denying their biological fatherhood of the children produced with their assistance. California now provides for the designation of three or more "parents" on its birth certificates.

The meaning of parent and child, like the meaning of husband and wife, is increasingly controlled by government.

The redefinition of marriage by the state turned the most effective limitation on government power, the family, into a creature of government. It does not matter whether this government takeover of private life is the work of elected representatives, unelected judges, or popular referendum. If government can define marriage and parenthood as it sees fit, the personal is the political, which is one of the definitions of tyranny.

A libertarian says redefining marriage and parenthood means more freedom. Now we can marry whom we wish and live as we wish rather than in accord with once-dominant social norms. But this freedom is fool's gold. It empowers the state, making government the source of our freedom. Courts and legislatures are commissioned to bulldoze whatever traditional limitations remain. No longer grounded in nature or custom, as the nation's Founders presumed, freedom becomes a creature of the political process—and thus vulnerable should power shift one way or another. Our rights are made by men, which means freedom is political. Again, this is one of the definitions of tyranny.

The libertarian's freedom also affords greater scope for the bad choices that, as we have seen, poor and working-class Americans are increasingly prone to make. The price of this freedom in the black community is criminality, mass incarceration, low educational attainment, and high unemployment. The problems are not yet as severe among working-class and middle-class whites, but the spreading dysfunction will require ever-greater government intervention to remediate the consequences. In a nation of personal freedom unhindered by moral norms and strong social customs—especially in matters of sex, children, and family—the administrative and therapeutic state expands. Without the guardrails of a strong culture of marriage, the interventions of social workers, welfare officials, and police officers provide regulation and support. Political power replaces moral authority.

Under the old moral system of restricted code and positional control, being a good father was an honorable achievement. The honorable man might be poor and uneducated, but the moral code gave him social standing, a sense of earned dignity. As a good father and faithful husband, he was any man's equal. The repudiation of that moral code has given us expanded personal freedom, but at every turn the power of government grows. Over the long term, we'll never succeed in limiting government unless we restore the moral authority of marriage.

LIMITING FROM ABOVE

Marriage and family limit government power from below; religion limits it from above. Faith makes a claim—an ultimate claim—on our loyalty. The church, synagogue, and mosque are sacred communities with laws of their own. When Caesar's law contradicts the law of God, divine authority trumps it. This is the most powerful of all limits on government.

Political power sometimes claims to rule in the name of God, purporting to wield his plenary authority. But Christianity, properly understood, drives a wedge between the city of man and the city of God. Emphasizing the fundamental distinction between secular and sacred politics, Jesus told Pontius Pilate, the representative of the greatest power of the ancient world, "My kingdom is not of this world." Secular powers rightly occupy themselves with protecting and securing our worldly wellbeing: security at the very least, prosperity and justice if we're fortunate. The church, by contrast, orders the lives of believers toward the salvation of their souls, transcending our worldly concerns. Christians therefore recognize the legitimate independence of the secular realm. Civic government is not and should not be absorbed into the church. In that sense, Christianity opposes theocracy. Even when the pope was sovereign of the Papal States, the church distinguished between his temporal and his spiritual authority.

This does not mean that worldly politics is of no interest to Christians. In his letter to the Romans, St. Paul writes that temporal authority is delegated by God to earthly rulers to restrain and punish wrongdoing. St. Augustine, taking a narrow view of that authority, held that secular power achieves, at best, a negative peace that keeps violence at bay, while a more optimistic St. Thomas Aquinas thought secular power capable of promoting justice. Across this range of prudential judgment, Christians exhort, criticize, and intervene in the civic affairs of their societies.

Our fellow citizens often resent this involvement, sometimes for good reasons. But on the whole, it's for the best. Christianity's aggressive role in American public life ensures that political power is hectored and hemmed in. The transcendent authority of the Bible is not a threat to democracy, as some secular liberals would have us believe. It's a crucial limit on worldly power.

In a totalitarian system, all aspects of life are absorbed into the political. The same thing can happen in a democracy if we recognize no authority higher than the will of the majority. It's no accident that the Declaration of Independence defines our basic rights as endowed by God. As such, they are "unalienable" bulwarks against tyranny. If their origin is not divine, then they are only as secure as the regime finds convenient.

Americans' conviction that our basic rights are God-given has been seriously eroded. When the chief justice of the Alabama supreme court resisted the imposition on his state of same-sex marriage by a federal court, arguing that courts have no authority to meddle with fundamental rights bestowed by God, he was roundly mocked in the press. Our rights, the journalists seemed to believe, are based in the political process itself. If that's the case, then they can be taken away as easily as they are given, redefined in accord with the spirit of the age. The subjection of everything to politics puts freedom in peril.

Appeals to natural law carry little or no weight today. During the years of debate about same-sex marriage, I argued, along with other Christians, that the difference between men and women has moral meaning, as does the reproductive potential of their sexual union. This was laughed out of court. Nature itself no longer defines our rights, nor does it impose a limit on what can be done through politics.

We should not despair when our arguments fail to persuade—or are summarily dismissed as "theological." Religion has a deeper strength and influence in public life. The sheer weight of Christianity—a community with its own laws, principles, and purposes, a sacred city whose supernatural character will not permit it to be absorbed into the city of man—counters the tendency of the political to become omnipotent. The "stubbornness" of faith is one of the few reliable limits on government.

The American Founders, appreciating the disruptive power of religious faith, prudently put the state at arm's length from theological controversy. The Bill of Rights prohibits the establishment of a national state religion and guarantees the free exercise of religion. But the denial of "the Laws of Nature and of Nature's God" as the source of our fundamental rights and the basis of justice is now bringing religious freedom into question. If our laws of marriage admit of no limitations from God or nature, why should *anything* be allowed to stand in the way of sheer political power? There is a clear trend to reduce the autonomy of Christian institutions, which in their "anti-science," "anti-gay," and "anti-woman" obscurantism have become intolerable obstacles to the kind of "progress" progressives desire.

The Obama administration signaled a new level of hostility toward religious freedom in 2011 when it urged the Supreme Court to discard a long-established protection of religious institutions' discretion in their appointment of ministers. The so-called "ministerial exception" to employment discrimination laws, based on the religion clauses of the First Amendment, protects a church from state interference in its internal governance, including "the selection of those who will personify its beliefs."

The argument for overturning such a thoroughly settled principle of constitutional law was remarkably aggressive, going too far even for the most liberal justices, and the administration lost in a unanimous decision. Nevertheless, the Justice Department had opened a question that's not likely to go away: Why should religious institutions be able to thwart the government's efforts to prevent employment discrimination and other injustices? It's an arresting question, given today's campaigns for sexual liberation. Gay marriage is now a civil right. Why should its vindication be stymied by religious doctrines? And what about transgender rights?

The domination of our society by governmental and quasi-governmental agencies that regulate, accredit, and certify a great deal of public life is putting religious liberty under pressure. The Department of Health and Human Services' contraception mandate (a result of Obamacare) has forced private businesses and religious institutions to defend the rights of conscience and religious freedom in lengthy and expensive legal battles with the federal government. The agency that accredits Gordon College in Massachusetts threatened to withdraw the evangelical school's accreditation if it did not change certain policies governing faculty, student, and staff behavior—policies about sex and marriage based on traditional Christian teaching. After a national controversy, the accreditors eventually backed off—for the time being. Catholic adoption agencies in Illinois, Massachusetts, and elsewhere have not been so lucky. State laws giving gay persons the right to adopt children have made no accommodation for agencies that for religious reasons will place children only in homes with a mother and a father.

The core issue in these controversies is the definition of who and what enjoys the right of religious freedom. Is a religious college, school, or charity entitled to the same protection as a church? Are the religious beliefs of entrepreneurs and company owners protected by the Constitution? Who gets to decide if an accommodation or exemption burdens religious freedom, the government or the churches?

How we answer these and other questions will determine whether religious institutions in America, especially Christian ones, remain a strong presence in society. The left increasingly speaks of freedom of "worship" or "belief," avoiding the broader formulation of the Constitution itself, the free "exercise" of religion. Our houses of worship remain independent, as do our inner lives. Nobody is saying we can't pray as we please in private. But what of religious practice more broadly? Jesus doesn't tell us only to lift up our voices in prayer and thanksgiving when we're inside a church. He commands us to seek out our neighbor and serve him. Are the terms and conditions of that service—a core element of the Christian life—something government can accredit, certify, and regulate just as it does banking or international trade? Is the Sermon on the Mount subject to government regulation?

As religious freedom is constricted, government power advances. As it expands, government power is limited. The institutional freedom of the churches, therefore, is decisively important for our political culture. Apple, General Electric, and other giant corporations are creatures of government, owing their existence to our laws of incorporation and contract. They can be hobbled by regulation, strangled by taxation, or simply nationalized. That's not true of the Christian churches and other religious communions, which existed before modern nation-states came into being. They can be harassed by hostile governments but cannot be controlled or destroyed, as the underground church in China demonstrates.

The seemingly all-powerful state meets a powerful counterforce in religious institutions. The churches have no legislative authority in American public life, but they have something more important—the solidarity of men and women joined in their obedience to God's will, resistant to control and domination by secular powers. Lives organized around God's Word are the surest bulwark against the tyranny of the political, the greatest danger of the democratic era. We serve the cause of freedom best by deepening our faith and standing firm in our convictions.

Young people are attracted to libertarianism, a philosophy that exalts individual freedom and promises to restrain the power of the state. It's tempting to explain this popularity as a symptom of youthful delusions of eternal self-sufficiency. But this interpretation largely misreads the libertarian impulse, for it is by no means limited to twenty-something males who think they are immortal and will never need anyone. Many young people today see libertarianism as a defense against establishment liberalism.

They know that so-called progressive thinking has constructed a vast politico-cultural complex that regulates everything from daily transactions in the marketplace to the words we're allowed to use in personal conversation. Having run the gauntlet of admission to elite universities, they experience the penetrating, tyrannical ambitions of political correctness when they arrive. Libertarianism protests against a lifetime of regulated existence.

They're right to want to restore freedom, but they're wrong to seek refuge in libertarianism, a false view of freedom that leaves us more, not less, vulnerable to political domination and bureaucratic management. In 1970, 40 percent of American households were constituted by married couples with children. That's now fallen to less than 20 percent. This simple statistic tells us what we already know: American society has been atomized by a cultural revolution that has undermined the authority of marriage as the presumptive norm for adult life. More than one-fifth of the American population no longer has an institutional religious affiliation, and American society no longer considers Christianity the primary source of public morality.

Libertarians see these changes as gains for freedom. No longer under the thumb of traditional marriage and religion, people can make up their own minds about how to live their personal lives, believing what they wish about religion and morality. Maybe so, but that's no basis for a free society. Codified rights offer limited protection. If the Supreme Court can find a right to same-sex marriage in the Constitution, then it can find anything, including dramatically different (and reduced) rights of speech, association, and religion. The most powerful limits to government power are found below and above political life: a strong culture of marriage and family, and robust, assertive religious institutions. A free society depends on strong family loyalties and faith's indomitable resolve.

CHAPTER 6

SEEK HIGHER THINGS

Our secular intellectuals have reached a dead end. They dismantle, deconstruct, critique, and unmask, leading us into an intellectual culture of knowingness that prides itself on never being duped, never succumbing to seductions, never becoming a slave of truths that, they say, are nothing more than yesterday's lies. There are no truths worthy of our loyalty, we are told. Higher education no longer promises something higher. Our universities encourage fear of error rather than desire for truth.

This makes ours a loveless era. There can be no love where there is no possibility of betrayal, no possibility of heartbreak. We cannot critique our way to an embrace. As the Dominican philosopher A. G. Sertillanges wrote, "Truth serves only her slaves." The critical intellect dissects the world, often a necessary and useful undertaking. But the way of love is greater, for it embraces truth and will not let it go. This embrace, this bond of loyalty and obedience to something higher, provides the true foundation for a culture of freedom.

Every society is weighed down by its false loves, and ours is no exception. Our hearth gods are health, wealth, and pleasure. Cigarette smoking among college students has fallen to all-time lows, surpassed by the use of marijuana. The god of health requires sacrifices that are compensated for by the beneficent ministrations of the god of pleasure. Middle-aged men and women force themselves out of bed and into the gym before work, where the scramble for wealth preoccupies them for sixty or eighty hours a week. Denying themselves sweets and fatty foods, they cultivate a taste for fine wines and locally produced cheese. This is how we live: asceticism by day and hedonism by night, giving each god its due in its season.

One clear sign of our bondage to these idols is the tenor of public debate. In his Cold War classic *The Suicide of the West*, James Burnham recognized that the struggle against communism was a metaphysical struggle over what it means to be human. He warned that Western liberalism had come to share the communists' materialism. I attended a symposium celebrating the fiftieth anniversary of Burnham's book, where I was struck by the extent to which the anti-metaphysical stance that Burnham identified in communism and rejected as inimical to a culture of freedom now characterizes what passes for conservatism. There was little interest in the metaphysical truths Burnham thought so essential. The speakers dwelt on the effect of tax rates on economic growth and the many defects of Obamacare. The only difference between the conservatism on display there and the liberalism Burnham feared was in their choice of policies for serving the gods of health, wealth, and pleasure.

Christians can debate among themselves about God, human nature, and the purpose of man, as well as with others. Jews and Muslims, and for that matter Marxists and liberals, have their own views. Some overlap with Christianity; others don't. The debate should be ongoing, and Christians need not win every argument. Even though revelation is trustworthy, we can err in our prudential judgments about how best to apply revealed truths, as the history of Christian culture shows. Moreover, metaphysical concepts can be elusive and are often colored by historical and cultural differences, making disagreements hard to pin down, much less resolve. But this debate about fundamental truths requires an underlying consensus. We cannot serve the common good unless we seek higher things. We must seek to order public life in accord with metaphysical truths higher than the ersatz ends of maximizing utility, encouraging dialogue, and promoting diversity.

SEEKING LOWER THINGS

The Swerve: How the World Became Modern by Stephen Greenblatt, an English professor at Harvard, recounts the discovery in 1417 by the humanist Poggio Bracciolini of Lucretius' philosophical epic *De rerum natura* (*On the Nature of Things*). Written a few decades before the time of Christ, this poem presents the materialist philosophy of the ancient Greek philosopher Epicurus to a Latin audience. Greenblatt's conceit is that this philosophy, known as Epicureanism and given such memorable poetic form by Lucretius and restored to Western readers by Poggio, revolutionized our conceptions of the meaning of life.

Honored with the National Book Award for nonfiction in 2011, *The Swerve* sports the usual features of high scholarship: endnotes, a long bibliography, and acknowledgements thanking professorial eminences. For the most part, however, the book is made up of clichés masquerading as history. Monks sit in dimly lit dungeons contemplating cruel disciplines that they can inflict upon themselves and others. For Christians, "Pleasure is a code name for vice." The medieval world loathed the body, repudiated erotic desire, etc., etc. On the other hand, Greenblatt's heroes, the Renaissance humanists, see through the hypocrisy and mendacity of Christianity. They are healthy men who enjoy life, retrieving from monastic libraries the surviving manuscripts of ancient literature, rediscovering a more humane pre-Christian past of genial pluralism, love of beauty, and an easy acceptance of pleasure. In the world of Greenblatt's imagination, Lucretius is a patron of "dangerous thoughts," his "essentially erotic" Epicurean philosophy reducing everything to the interplay of material atoms in an "inherently sexual" universe.

These caricatures are unfortunate, because Epicurus the philosopher and Lucretius the poet are important thinkers well worth serious consideration. Though today's adherents of a reductive materialism often appeal to the authority of "science" for their metaphysical claims, Epicurus and Lucretius understood and explained materialism's spiritual appeal. Studying them can help us understand why a reductive view of the human person appeals to moderns like Stephen Greenblatt, few of whom know or care much about science.

The Epicurean tenet that everything that exists is made up of atoms was not based on observation and experiment. The ancient materialists were attracted to atoms because they prized their simplicity or indivisibility (which is what "atom" means), as well as their indestructibility. Atoms are infinite in number and ceaselessly in motion, eternally combining in all sorts of configurations (such as you and me), breaking down, and reconfiguring.

Simplicity, indestructibility, infinity, and eternity suggest an invulnerability and deathlessness that ancient philosophers ascribed to the gods. Epicurus held that true happiness comes when we are godlike, that is, when we are as much like atoms as possible. We cannot achieve that indivisibility and indestructability in our physical existence. After all, we invariably suffer and eventually die. But he contended that we can make our consciousness indivisible and indestructible. The key to attaining this state of spiritual indestructibility is to cultivate imperturbability, or peace of mind. If Epicurus had given the Sermon on the Mount, he would have pronounced, "Blessed are those who are untroubled."

And how do we achieve that? Aren't we doomed to be upset when we're jilted by a lover or denied a cherished promotion? Won't we cry when someone we love dies? Aren't we worried about running out of money or failing to achieve our goals? No, taught Epicurus. If we adopt the right attitudes, we can achieve a godlike indifference to the difficulties of life.

"Waste not, want not" is an old maxim, but older still is "Want not, want not." Epicurus counseled careful discipline of desire. "If you wish to make Pythocles rich," he wrote of a friend, "do not add to his store of money, but subtract from his desires." True pleasure, according to Epicurus, is "the state wherein the body is free from pain and the mind from anxiety." We can be unperturbed and untroubled if we don't care about anything. If, to use the Buddhist term, we are non-attached, we can enjoy this Epicurean happiness.

Reducing our desire is easier said than done. Human beings are factories of desire: desire for sex, food, survival, glory, honor, and more. Epicurus's genius was to see the therapeutic value of materialism. The apparent meaninglessness of life might seem like bad news, but it detaches us from our desires. If nothing matters, then I can't be hurt when things don't go my way. After all, there is no "my way." It's just atoms doing their thing. Although it seems counterintuitive to those of us shaped by Christianity, materialism can be psychologically liberating.

On the Nature of Things was and remains compelling because the poet skillfully draws his readers into the desire-reducing therapy of materialism. Concerned about the fate of your soul? Have no fear, your soul is but a temporary configuration of atoms. Afraid of death? Remember that death is just part of the natural dissolution of all things. When you die you will not suffer, because when you die you will be no more. The atoms of which you are now constituted will simply go their aimless way to constitute something else.

Lucretius also recognized, perhaps more than Epicurus did, that our lives are agitated by cultural ideals. We're vulnerable to the opinion of others. We want to be honored and praised, and we shrink from shame and criticism. Don't be so foolish, he says, as to imagine that conquests and victories, honor and shame, praise and blame, make one bit of difference. Do the indivisible and eternal atoms care if Rome falls?

Culture not only stimulates and focuses our social instinct, it provides a powerful vocabulary of love. In a long and important passage, Lucretius takes aim at Venus's power to torment us with desire. The passion of lovers is "storm-tossed," he writes, inflicting the terrible pain of longing and anxious worries about betrayal. A thoroughgoing materialism can deliver us from these dangers by showing them to be illusory. If we realize that sex is just a bodily function, a matter of friction and not spiritual communion, we can free ourselves from love's threats to our tranquility of mind. And should we be smitten, Lucretius advises us "to lance the first wound with new incisions; to salve it, while it is still fresh, with promiscuous attachments." This seems like a hedonistic counsel, but it is not. Here as elsewhere, the therapy Lucretius prescribes is reductive. We remove existential threats when we make our experiences small and insignificant.

Modern liberalism promotes this Lucretian metaphysical modesty, insisting that peace and harmony are more likely if higher things are downplayed in public life. Liberals preach moral relativism not because they really believe that all truths are relative, but because they think downplaying truth is the best way to ease social relations in a diverse society. The intuition is simple and alluring: if nothing is worth fighting for, then nobody will fight. Epicurean wisdom softens existence: if nothing is worth worrying about, then we won't worry.

Liberals apply this same therapeutic debasement to personal life and moral ideals. Traditional cultures teach young people to sacrifice for high ideals, sometimes to the point of radical self-denial. Jesus tells the rich young man that his obedience to the moral law is not enough. If he seeks perfection, he must sell all he owns and give the proceeds to the poor. And even ordinary ideals involve sacrifice. Their sexual instincts draw men and women together, and paternal and maternal instincts bind them to their children, but the everyday obligations of sexual fidelity and parental responsibility can be burdensome, requiring genuine sacrifice. Here the spirit of the age goes to work, lowering our ideals until they become mere lifestyle choices.

The message is clear: there is no firm, higher truth about how to live. But the resulting meaninglessness, as Epicurus and Lucretius consolingly tell us, is a life-affirming message. For if nothing is worth sacrificing for, then nobody will need to make sacrifices. Instead of straining to fit ourselves into cultural and moral molds, we can just get on with life. We no longer need to live for the sake of higher truths. We can now live for the sake of…life.

In *The Great Gatsby*, F. Scott Fitzgerald depicts the indolent, troubled world of upper-crust young Americans during the Roaring Twenties. Tom Buchanan, a Yale graduate, represents a type: the arrogant young man who has inherited money. By his way of thinking, the white, northern races produce virile, strong, commanding men like himself, and they rightly rule. The mansion overlooking the Long Island Sound, the yellow Rolls-Royce, the trust fund—he believes he holds them in accord with the higher justice of racial evolution.

This pseudoscientific view, known as social Darwinism, was a convenient philosophy for American elites a century ago, allowing them to hold themselves exempt from the old constraints of duty and the Christian recognition that we are all equal in the eyes of God. It eased their consciences about their superordinate power and wealth. A materialist interpretation of life, bearing the authority of "science," was assumed to demonstrate that the old Christian principles of charity and more recent democratic ideals of equality are illusions. There are no ideals. The only truth about human beings is found in the never-ending evolutionary struggle for survival. So the question of justice answers itself: the winners are by definition those who should be winners.

Today, elites turn to Epicurean materialism rather than social Darwinism, which has been discredited. Stephen Greenblatt affirms the therapy of lowering and disenchantment: "Human insignificance—the fact that it is not all about us and our fate—is, Lucretius insisted, good news." What Greenblatt fails to see is that this gospel is for the rich and powerful—professors at Harvard, for example. As materialism disenchants, the norms by which we can hold the powerful accountable melt away.

I can't imagine a more convenient and reassuring philosophy for today's One Percent. The swirl of atoms has given them tenure at Harvard, a high income, power, status. It's not a matter of right or wrong. Like the social Darwinism and racial theories that eased the conscience of Fitzgerald's Tom Buchanan, Greenblatt's materialist philosophy reassures those who hold power today. Because nothing we do in this vast cosmos matters, the high and mighty can do what they want, and nobody can criticize them.

Materialism denies the existence of higher things, and relativism denies we could know about them even if they did exist. Both are therapies of lowering and disenchantment widely promoted today. But few people are entirely consistent. For most it's sufficient for strong truths to be sidelined. This can be done by way of a liberalism that rules out metaphysical claims as illiberal. Or the therapy of lowering can be pursued by a selective moral relativism and rhetoric of inclusion and tolerance. Our educational culture frequently employs this therapy with multiculturalism and political correctness. It allows teachers to shift attention away from questions of truth without engaging them.

These strategies serve the interests of the powerful. Lucretius's poem is colored by a spirit of rebellion against prevailing opinion, but Epicurus was more consistent. He counseled conformity to local custom, because materialism teaches that what we conform to doesn't matter one way or the other. It's not an accident that Epicureanism flourished during the imperial period of Roman rule. The lowering, disenchanting therapy helped educated Romans reconcile themselves to their political impotence. Today's middle class—increasingly dominated by the One Percent, who are transferring their loyalty to a globalized capitalist system that richly rewards them—are in the same position. The therapy of materialism helps them accept their political impotence. Needless to say, this acquiescence, promoted by our educational system, serves the interests of the One Percent.

Stephen Greenblatt applauds Lucretius's spirit of critique, "speaking the truth to power" as they say. But materialism is attractive to people like him because it justifies the status quo. There are no higher truths to serve. Accept things as they are, for they can't be otherwise. Far from revolutionary, materialism, like all the lowering therapies, eases the way for empire and servitude.

ENCHANTMENT

While Epicurus and Lucretius sought peace of mind by lowering their expectations, other ancient thinkers sought divine tranquility through enchantment, a ravishing of the soul by something higher. Plato made love the engine of knowledge. Truth reveals herself most fully to those who, like Socrates, desire nothing else. It is the Old Testament, however, that most clearly makes love the lynchpin of human flourishing: "You shall love the LORD your God with all your heart and with all your soul, and with all your might."

Wisdom, argues the book of Proverbs, requires matrimony. "Love her," we are told, "and she will keep you; she will honor you if you embrace her" (4:8). Wisdom builds herself a beautiful house, adorns herself, and prepares a festive meal. We do not defeat foolishness and falsehood with critiques that free us from error, and we certainly don't find peace of mind through non-attachment. It is the power of love that overcomes the prostitution of our hearts and minds. "Come," she calls to us, "eat of my bread and drink the wine I have mixed."

The early Christian tradition adopted the way of love and the therapy of enchantment without reservation, often explicitly as an alternative to the contemporary philosophies that encouraged people to accept their impotence and submit to the status quo. St. Augustine in his *Confessions* famously declared, "Our hearts are restless until they find their rest in thee." Our tendency is to read this metaphorically, but Augustine meant it literally. Like Epicurus and Lucretius, he knew how painful it is to be buffeted by desires, especially those that seem insatiable. His desire to rest in God initially produced not tranquility but what he described as "burning" and "turning endlessly," attached as he was to his sins,

worried about his reputation and fearful that he could not endure
the renunciation of his sinful habits.

Pining for God and yet unable to surrender to him, Augustine
longed for rest. A crucial section of his *Confessions* tells of the
days and hours before his conversion. He recounts anguished
moments of inner turmoil made worse by his intense desire to
rest in the truth of Christ. To rest in Christ—or to use the language of the Gospel of John, to abide in him—this desire parallels
the Epicurean goal of tranquility or peace of mind. The critical
difference, however, is that Augustine and the Christian tradition
as a whole seek stability, tranquility, and peace of mind not
through non-attachment but through love fulfilled. "Let my
bones be penetrated by your love," Augustine prays with an ardor
that evokes the profound desire that suffuses the Song of Songs.
His prayer is answered. After his conversion he writes, "You
pierced my heart with the arrow of your love."

Augustine's reference to the divine arrow of love evokes the
pagan image of Cupid's arrows, symbols of love's enslaving
power. This erotic image had already been spiritualized in pagan
thought. Philosophy—love of wisdom—turns to love's binding
power, installing truth as the soul's sovereign. Augustine's image
of the arrow of divine love fuses pagan philosophy's emphasis on
love's erotic, soul-controlling power to the Old Testament image
of matrimony, representing the soul's union with God. A penetrating, all-commanding love, made stable in matrimonial fidelity, cures Augustine's restless, troubled soul. "Suddenly," he
writes, "it had become sweet to me to be without the sweets of

folly. What I had once feared to lose was now a delight to dismiss." As a fire clears the field of weeds, the fierce heat of love burns away his distracting, dissipating worldly desires, bringing him to rest in Christ. It is a paradox, but not an unfamiliar one. The hot, driving passion of love makes us stable, which is to say, tranquil. Under love's enchantment we become devoted to that which we love. Our hearts rest in the beloved.

Love and her enchantments can be dangerous. Our loves may be false and our ardor misguided. The twentieth century tells a sad, blood-soaked tale of perverse ideologies passionately believed. Love is never self-authenticating. It must be purified, sometimes by reason, sometimes by conscience, sometimes by God's authority.

Purified or not, however, love works in a way completely different from that of Epicurean materialism and other lowering therapies, such as critique and the hermeneutics of suspicion. It does not make us immune to the perils of life through a cultivated indifference. The spirit of love is one of commitment. Wedding vows recklessly venture permanence: for richer for poorer, in sickness and in health, to love and cherish, till death us do part. The same is true of a patriotic love or the love of any human thing. The way of enchantment stakes out territory, steeling us to defend it, promising us that love's power is greater than any setback or disappointment.

Even more demanding is the supernatural love of God. The saints—Olympians of love—are not patrons of indifference. Their Christian tranquility is far more arrogant than the peace of mind sought by Epicurus and Lucretius. "O death," St. Paul asks with haughty disdain, "where is thy sting? O grave, where is thy victory?" Christian faith encourages a worldly otherworldliness, not an Epicurean (and postmodern) otherworldly worldliness. To disenchant life, to behold all things through the eyes of critical reason—these therapies of lowering may free us from the pains of desire, but they are dry, cold, and loveless, leaving the world as it is. Christianity's vision of peace encourages us to hope that the sinews of life—our very bones—can be penetrated by an enduring, unconquerable, eternalizing love. Love's enchantments give us places to stand in a cruel and unreliable world: next to my wife, with my compatriots, before my God. Like a boulder in the midst of a stream, this stable love alters the course of history.

FALSE FREEDOM

Justice Anthony Kennedy's majority opinion in *Obergefell v. Hodges,* the decision finding a constitutional right to gay marriage, opens with a grand statement about freedom: "The Constitution promises liberty to all within its reach, a liberty that includes specific rights that allow persons, within a lawful realm, to define and express their identity." Add to this a truism of our age—that homosexual desires constitute an "identity"—and the decision follows as a matter of logic. The Constitution's promise of liberty requires us to redefine marriage so that people with homosexual desires can "express their identity." This way of thinking about freedom has the upper hand today, but it is dishonest. Through an equivocal use of "identity," Kennedy relies on the cogency of a classical account of freedom while substituting a postmodern one.

One side of the equivocation suggests that my identity is more than my will or free choice. It's what is essential to me, and a just society provides me the freedom to live in accord with my essential identity. If we allow that human beings have a distinct nature, then freedom is the ability to live in accord with that nature. This is the classical view, the view of both the ancient Greek and the Christian traditions. It's also the view presumed by the Founders, who took it for granted that since we are rational animals, genuine freedom must include the liberty to make and consider arguments, even disruptive arguments, about justice, morality, and how we should live together in society. The constitutional rights of free speech and a free press—at times interpreted expansively, at other times less so—protect that liberty, acknowledging man's identity as a rational animal.

We're also social and religious animals, and in the United States we enjoy constitutional rights of association and religion that protect these aspects of our humanity. European nations have not always accorded religion as much elbow room as it enjoys in America, but there is a common recognition that religious animals must be free to worship in accord with their most profound convictions. Pre-modern European societies accorded special rights to universities, guilds, and free cities, recognizing that social animals have distinct loyalties that must be given public expression. Marriage itself is the most basic mode of social bonding. It's no coincidence, therefore, that the Christian tradition has always insisted that free consent is necessary for a valid marriage. Our social nature is frustrated rather than fulfilled when we are herded into artificial aggregates. Genuine social life requires a margin of freedom for us to choose our associations.

The problem is that in Justice Kennedy's formulation, "identity" is not the "human nature" of classical philosophy. He is talking about something I can *define* rather than an essential part of who I am. "Identity" understood in this way is not something to be acknowledged or protected by freedom; it's just another word for freedom itself. Kennedy's formulation, then, is an empty tautology: the promise of liberty is the right to liberty. Freedom means living in accord with freedom.

This shell game is just one instance of the dishonesty widespread in cultural liberalism. We are told that homosexuality is an inborn trait, an essential part of a person's makeup. At the same time, identity is plastic and open-ended, something to be discovered, even invented. LGBTQ today, who-knows-what tomorrow. The contradiction is patent. When it suits progressives, they play up the fixed nature of identity, allowing them to draw upon classical ideals of freedom. Then, when that becomes constricting, they toggle over to the flexible, self-defined meaning of identity. We're told that individuals must be free to *construct* their own identities and that it's oppressive to think otherwise.

And so liberals have it both ways, as we've often experienced. If we call homosexual acts immoral, we're failing to respect something essential about gay people. If we presume to define what is essential about anyone, including gay people, we're encroaching upon their freedom to define their identities. Identity is essential—and arbitrary. It's the foundation for freedom—and a product of free choices. Heads they win, tails we lose.

A similar self-contradiction is also common among moral relativists and other proponents of lowering therapies. All truth is relative, they say, insisting on the truth of their relativism. Preaching a universe without purpose, they take it as their overriding purpose to convert others to the view that there is no purpose.

The contradictions go deep. Many a modern liberal knows that the identity politics he acquiesces to, and even at times endorses, are illiberal. Most regret the dead hand of political correctness, yet they are unable to denounce it and rarely defend its victims. Some recognize the brutality of abortion, but they cannot turn against our regime of "choice." Most suspect that being male and female matters—but they are unable to stand against the sexual politics that say otherwise.

American culture is stuck in any number of dead ends, many of them falsely labeled as roads to freedom. I have argued in earlier chapters that the dominant ethic of nonjudgmentalism accords important advantages to the One Percent. Nonjudgmentalism is part of the secular liberal culture that sees identity as something we can define—for ourselves, but not for others (that would be judgmental). This culture of permission combined with censure of those who do not obey the new rules for a world without moral rules allows our ruling class to compliment itself as morally progressive. It provides the added benefit of a therapeutic moral vocabulary with which to denounce populist challenges to their power. "Mrs. Johnson, I'm afraid the sorts of views you've expressed about sex and marriage can be very hurtful."

Pointing this out rarely convinces my opponents, I find, but pointing out error is important nevertheless. Doing so may cause those with whom we disagree to hesitate. We can embarrass and fluster with well-formulated refutations. It's even possible to induce second thoughts. But we rarely convince. That's because the deepest mental poverty of our time is one of imagination and courage, not reason and intelligence. Today's so-called progressives, persevering in self-contradiction, are all too human. When we can't imagine alternatives, most of us remain loyal to the ideas that dominate our minds, even when we know they're false. We can change our minds only when we are able to envision a more powerful truth. We need to see the true currency of freedom in order to free ourselves from its counterfeit.

TRUE FREEDOM

In the Old Testament there are two straightforward words for freedom. *Chofesh* is used in Exodus 21:2, which stipulates that a male Hebrew slave is to be freed after six years of service. (The same word, incidentally, appears in modern Israel's national anthem, evoking the hope that Jews will be a free people in their own land.) *Dror* is used in Leviticus 25:10, which commands that during the Jubilee year freedom shall be proclaimed to all the inhabitants of the land. The same word appears in Isaiah 61:1, which prophesizes that the Anointed One will bind up the broken-hearted and proclaim liberty to the captives. But for the Passover rites, the ancient rabbis settled on another word for the deliverance from slavery commemorated in that celebration—*herut*—and that is the word most Jews associate with freedom.

This is more than a little strange. *Herut* appears in 1 Kings 21:8, where it is translated as "elders" or "ministers," those dedicated to God's service, hardly a meaning that brings the concept of freedom to mind. But things get stranger still. In Exodus 32:16, we find the word *harut*, which means to carve or engrave, in the account of Moses's descent from Mount Sinai with the two stone tablets of the Ten Commandments. In the absence of vowel markings in the biblical Hebrew, the rabbinic tradition says that here one should read not *harut* but *herut*. "Engrave" really means "dedicate," which really means "freedom."

Verbal tricks of this sort are common in rabbinic teaching. Unlike Christianity, which defines doctrines in explicit terms, commonly drawing on philosophical concepts, Judaism often articulates its doctrines in provocative and sometimes counterintuitive interpretations of biblical verses or laws. In this case, a seeming misreading of Exodus 32:16 provides a definition of freedom. To be truly free, as the rabbis teach in their substitution of *herut* for *harut*, we must engrave God's commandments on our hearts—a view of freedom, as Rabbi Jonathan Sacks points out, implied in the divine promise in Jeremiah 31:33: "I will put my law within them, and I will write it on their hearts."

This view of freedom is carried into the New Testament. Jeremiah 31:33 is quoted in Hebrews 8:10, and St. Paul evokes it in 2 Corinthians 3:3 when he calls the saints "a letter from Christ delivered by us, written not with ink but with the Spirit of the living God, not on tablets of stone but on tablets of human hearts." This, then, is the freedom for which Christ has set us free: to have the law of Christ engraved on our hearts. His way is the perfect law, which is the law of liberty (James 1:25). The greater our loyalty to his way, the more we enter into true freedom. The more perfect our obedience, the more perfect our liberty.

This seems paradoxical to the modern mind. How can loyalty and obedience be the basis for freedom? Isn't freedom being able to do what we want?

Yes, precisely.

Genuine freedom is difficult to achieve, because it's not so easy to do what we want. There are powers in the world that wish us to do as *they* want, making it hard to remain stable in our own purposes. Consider how wealthy, well-educated parents communicate fear and anxiety to their children these days. Freed from the day-to-day struggle for survival that characterizes life for so many throughout the world, they are nevertheless filled with concern for the success of their children. They expend tremendous energy on choosing just the right private schools and tutors, and admission to a noted university is a life-or-death matter. In spite of their wealth and status, these parents feel compelled to run their children through the gauntlet of merito-cratic competition. There remains little room for freedom. If that's the lot of the rich, what hope for freedom do middle-class and poor people have in the face of far more immediate eco-nomic and social pressures?

The ability to stand firm against worldly powers is the founda-tion of freedom. If we cannot be moved, we cannot be controlled. If we can resist domination, we are indomitable. The freest man is the one who can spit in the eye of those who imagine themselves all-powerful, asserting, "I will *not.*" We are most fully free when we can say with St. Paul, "I am sure that neither death, nor life, nor angels, nor principalities, nor things present, nor things to come, nor powers, nor height, nor depth, nor anything else in all creation, will be able to separate us from the love of God in Christ Jesus our Lord" (Romans 8:38–39). The martyrs testify to this freedom in a particularly powerful way.

There are natural analogies to the supernatural freedom of faith. Aleksandr Solzhenitsyn did not start out with a Christian faith. He was a faithful communist. But a higher loyalty inter-vened, a loyalty to the truth about the human person. A collision with the Soviet regime's ideological falsification of reality was inevitable, but as a political prisoner Solzhenitsyn was able to remain anchored to truth. His convictions gave him no guns to fight back with, but they led him on a courageous campaign of truth-telling that both depended on and strengthened his own interior freedom of thought. He nurtured the same freedom in his readers. "A word of truth outweighs the world," he declared in accepting the Nobel Prize for literature.

His courage and gifts as a writer may have been unique, but Solzhenitsyn's experiences of freedom are commonplace. Many men have overcome the natural bondage to fear out of loyalty— loyalty to their nation or a philosophy, perhaps, or simply to a small band of comrades. Ordinary fathers and mothers often rise to heroic heights in defense of their children. Paternal or maternal love frees them from bondage to their selfish desires. A binding love empowers. The rabbis were right about freedom, about *herut*. What's engraved on our hearts strengthens our spines.

After an escape from the Nazi concentration camp at Auschwitz, a commander selected at random ten prisoners to be put to death in retaliation. When one of the ten cried out, "My wife! My children!" another prisoner, the Polish Franciscan Maximilian Kolbe, stepped forward and said, "Take me instead." It was not a moment he had rehearsed, but he seized it with an act of *herut* in a death camp designed to stamp out every trace of freedom. Because he could stand firm in Christ, he could step forward.

Those most deeply bound to others in love are the freest to face the future without illusions, and love's enslaving devotion makes them most able to exercise responsibility to shape the future.

RESTORING A CULTURE OF FREEDOM

Many Americans today lack a place to stand. There are fewer enduring loves and demanding loyalties. The marketplace encourages us to consider our self-interest. Families are less stable. And in the background, a perpetual critique whines that nothing is worth our loyalty. The family, Freud reveals, is not a refuge in a cruel world but a factory of psychological distress. Marx, Nietzsche, and Foucault unmask religion as an opiate and patriotism as a fool's game. Reason is power's favorite mask, and loyalty to truth makes one an unwitting pawn of oppressing forces that are always operating beneath the surface. These are the sorts of things we're told again and again.

So we are less free, even as freedom is on everyone's lips. The anxious and helpless can't face the future on their own, confident in their freedom. They need support and reassurance, which we should provide. But as we try to meet that need, let's not lose sight of the deeper impoverishment, the loss of freedom. What's needed most today are renewed loves and loyalties, not an extension of the Nanny State.

Marriage is an obvious place to start. Although gravely weakened by cohabitation, divorce, and now same-sex marriage, it remains for most people a powerful experience of *herut*. Wedding vows engrave an enduring fidelity on our hearts, bringing *real* freedom. Families offer stubborn resistance not only to the intrusions of the administrative state but also to the imperial penetration of mass culture into every aspect of our lives. The dinner table is under the mother's and father's authority, not the government's, not Hollywood's, not the *New York Times*'.

It's no accident that the decline of marriage over the last few decades corresponds with a growth of government. In part that's because the family—closely attuned to its members' needs and motivated not to waste resources—is a highly efficient welfare system. When it breaks down, something has to take its place, and these days that's the government. But more importantly, marriage gives men and women a place to stand.

To restore a culture of freedom, we need to rebuild the culture of marriage, for marriage and family are the source of our most common and most powerful natural loves and loyalties. Stronger still are the supernatural bonds of faith, so religious renewal is central to freedom's renewal. This does not necessarily mean evangelizing the unchurched, though it's good to do so. More important, perhaps, will be the deepening of our own faith, engraving on our hearts what we affirm with our lips.

Unlike the state, the church and synagogue have no armies, no police, no prisons. Religious institutions lack the sophistication and reach of Big Media and the analytic power of Big Data. They don't pay high salaries or offer rich dividends. What they have is more powerful. Faith provides us with a place to stand, setting us aflame with the urgency of obedience to God's will. Sometimes these flames have turned religious communities into fierce champions of divine causes, fomenting insurrections and pulling down governments, but as a rule, the power of religious communities comes from their *herut*, what is engraved on their hearts. The freedom of faith is not the product of laws, constitutions, or international declarations of human rights. It comes from invincible obedience to God's will that makes it impossible for secular powers to control the church and synagogue.

We see this freedom at work in the debates about marriage. There's nothing uniquely biblical about the view that marriage is between a man and a woman, and no one needs religion to understand why transgenderism is ultimately inhuman. But today it is almost only religious people who are speaking up against the ideological mutilation of marriage, sex, and the family. It seems we alone are free.

Many are engaged in important efforts to protect our constitutional liberties. They're right to defend freedom of speech, freedom of the press, freedom of assembly, and, today especially, freedom of religion. But in this time and in this place, *herut* matters more—much more. Religious believers' capacity to resist legal coercion and social pressure will preserve liberty for everyone and will do so more effectively than legislation and favorable judicial decisions. For as we stand strong, the vulnerable can live in our leeward side, as it were, protected by our boldness of speech and refusal to be coerced. The one child who stands up to the bully secures freedom for the whole schoolyard.

Herut does not just protect; it inspires. We should not underestimate how acutely our fellow citizens feel their bondage. An evangelical friend of mine, a young professor at a large state university, has spoken out against gay marriage. Most of his students are first-generation college students. Some are illegal immigrants. Justice Kennedy's definition of liberty as the freedom to define and express one's own identity mocks them. Uncertain how they will pay their rent or tuition, they have little sense of control over their lives. A middle-class life with a decent salary and a stable marriage is an "identity" they'd welcome. This professor's public stances against gay marriage have, predictably, brought him a great deal of grief. He's been attacked on social media. Activist groups work to get him fired. Nearly all his students are in favor of gay marriage. Yet his courses are full and popular. His students respect him, even admire him. They see in him real convictions. He has a place to stand that allows him to resist domination and to take possession of his life. It's a strength that makes him free as they too wish to be free.

Having forsaken higher things, we undermine the basis for freedom. We think that what people lack is money, when the rich themselves are enslaved to the meritocratic machine of their own invention. Our secular high priests preach materialism, but it's a counsel of compliance, not freedom. We offer people the opportunity to define their own identities, imagining that it's the next stage of social justice. It's the opposite, for the false freedom of our progressive elites leaves ordinary people undefended against their own unreliable instincts and a crude, invasive mass culture. At nearly every turn, people are subjected to lowering therapies, convincing them that there are no higher things worth serving. Our secular culture disempowers because it gives people nothing to love and thus no place to stand.

A Christian society nurtures in its citizens a desire for higher things. It prizes love and loyalty over intelligence and achievement. It honors devotion over a supposed critical independence. It offers enchantment, not disenchantment. A Christian society does not compel faith or install priests in positions of public authority. But it affirms that we are fully human and more genuinely free when we give ourselves to something higher.

A Christian society fulfills the American dream of freedom because it empowers people. The proclamation of Christ gives his followers a place to stand, stability in a truth that cannot be conquered. A Christian society will have non-Christians. Not everyone will abide in Christ. But at its best, a Christian society encourages *herut*, the true, enduring freedom that allows ordinary people—little people—to take possession of their lives. *Herut* is the freedom born of a higher love that allows us to stand up to worldly powers that claim dominion over our lives.

CHAPTER 7

The Possibility of a Christian Society

America feels less Christian today than ever before. In a 1957 government survey, only 3 percent of Americans said they had no religious affiliation. In a 2008 survey, that figure had grown to 17 percent. This demographic cohort, known as the "Nones" (because they check "none" when asked their religious affiliation), continues to increase. More recent surveys put them at 20 percent of the population and more than 30 percent among young people.

Given this trend, resurrecting a Christian society is a pipe dream, isn't it? I'm not so sure. The rise of the Nones does not indicate a significant drop in churchgoing. A half-century ago, a quarter of the American population, perhaps more, never (or hardly ever) went to church. They were functionally Nones. In the 1950s, however, the social atmosphere was quite different. Nearly everyone felt social pressure to identify as religious, which in America meant Christian. People described themselves as Methodist or Presbyterian even though they did not attend services. We were a Christian nation in a sociological sense. America was part of Christendom, and in Christendom everyone is Christian, even those who aren't.

Christendom is no more. Those who don't go to church now feel free to say that they have no religion, or more accurately no "organized" religion. Bookstores feature shelves of volumes on spirituality. Most Nones believe in God, or at least in some kind of higher power. There's a great deal of latitude for a do-it-yourself approach to life's ultimate questions. Fifty or sixty years ago, it would have been unimaginable for a schoolteacher in Des Moines to be open and unapologetic about having no connection to Christianity. Today it's perfectly acceptable.

This marks an important change in our culture, to be sure, yet the end of Christendom has not meant the end of Christianity. In regular surveys by the federal government since World War II, about 35 percent of Americans have said they attend services at least once a week. Studies in which people keep daily logs of their activities—generally more accurate—suggest that weekly attendance is closer to 25 percent. In either case, church attendance has been remarkably consistent for decades—and perhaps, as some scholars speculate, for the past hundred years. These people are the committed core, the Christian leaven in society.

I do not want to underplay the end of Christendom. Christians no longer have a monopoly on moral leadership. In many areas, we've been pushed to the margins, despised as culture warriors or bigots because of our views about sexual morality. Nevertheless, there are *plenty* of Christians in America, more than enough to renew the Christian character of our society. There's as much leaven today as there was in 1955, and probably as much as there was in 1905.

Moreover, we don't need to restore old-style American Christendom. The ways of God are not the ways of man. Spiritual power is not the same as worldly power. The Lord puts down the mighty from their seat and exalts the humble and meek. We are living in a season of anti-establishment fervor, and that means there are evangelical advantages to being on the periphery rather than at the center. Given the enduring strength of Christian practice and the weaknesses of our secular establishment, I see no reason why the Christian character of America can't be renewed.

THE NEW CULTURE WARRIORS

In the fall of 1959, the *Harvard Crimson* noted that an education at America's most illustrious university, founded to train the Congregational clergy of New England, "actually seems detrimental to Protestantism, since over 26 percent of the students born in this religion have since rejected it." Today, of course, no one would think this a subject worth mentioning, since "the stock of the Puritans" is nowhere to be seen at fair Harvard, populated as it now is by Nones.

Harvard reflects a general trend. Until fairly recently, our society was dominated by White Anglo-Saxon Protestants—WASPs. The term is redundant—show me an Anglo-Saxon who isn't white—and also a bit of a misnomer. Some of the richest and most powerful men of the early twentieth century were Scotch-Irish, not Anglo-Saxon. People of German, Dutch, and French Huguenot descent were also prominent; Roosevelt is not an Anglo-Saxon name. But we live at a distance from Europe, and in the American context the term encompasses all Protestants of Northern European descent.

Well into the second half of the twentieth century, WASPs reigned supreme, holding the most important corporate, financial, government, and university positions. The rest of American society accepted this predominance. Celebrities of Jewish, Italian, and Eastern European descent adopted WASP stage names: Jack Benny, George Burns, Rock Hudson, Dean Martin.

Protestantism, of course, put the "P" in WASP. The Methodist, Presbyterian, Episcopal, and Congregational churches shaped the Christian consensus that dominated America. "Mainline" Protestantism was liberal—not in the narrow, political sense but in its broader meaning. A liberal Protestant could be a political conservative or a follower of FDR. For a WASP, liberality in religion meant doctrinal flexibility, moral earnestness, and confidence that American progress was part of God's greater plan for mankind.

It's easy to dismiss the liberal Christianity of mainline Protestantism as theologically compromised, even heretical, but we mustn't discount the good it did. Those acquainted only with the political culture of the past few decades, in which religious conservatives have been at odds with secular liberals, may not realize that mainline Protestantism initiated and led most of the progressive movements in American history. The civil rights movement is only the most recent example. Abolitionism was a church-based political movement. More than one hundred years ago, the Social Gospel challenged the social Darwinism that was popular among the rich and powerful. Christian progressivism did a great deal to prepare the American capitalist class to accept, and even in some cases support, the modern welfare state. Liberal Protestants led the most ambitious effort of social engineering in American history, Prohibition; promoted pacifism, disarmament, and world government after World War I; and defined America's role as defender of the free world during the Cold War.

By 1960, although mainline Protestantism seemed as influential as ever, it had become superficial, and within a decade it was in catastrophic decline. Nevertheless, despite the collapse of their churches, the WASP elite themselves and their other institutions have not collapsed. Harvard, for instance, is more powerful today than it was in 1959 when the *Crimson* noticed that its Protestantism was evaporating. Furthermore, the wealthy, powerful WASPs who once worshipped at socially prominent Presbyterian or Episcopal churches have not disappeared. Like Harvard, they are richer and more powerful than ever. True, they have stopped going to church, but through their WASP institutions, which continue to set the standard for "elite," they have coopted other ethnic groups, white and nonwhite, instilling in them the post-Protestant WASP worldview. The *New York Times* is owned by a Jewish family, and its editors and reporters come from many different backgrounds, but the "newspaper of record" is an entirely reliable organ of post-Protestant WASP culture.

The reinvention of the WASP has brought about a powerful new leadership class that, for the first time in American history, has no vital connection to Christianity. It is filled with post-Protestant WASPs, men and women who are not necessarily Anglo-Saxon, certainly aren't Protestant, and sometimes aren't white, but who have been formed by America's WASP establishment. Like Harvard, these institutions initially evolved into their present forms under WASP control, which ensured a continuity of sensibility and outlook that has been sustained and even strengthened by a an outwardly more diverse leadership.

While the old WASP culture justified its supereminence on the basis of historical pedigree, the new WASPs make no hereditary claim, relying instead on a justification more compatible with the American democratic ideal and dream of freedom—they are the product of a meritocracy. But the new WASPs share with the old a bedrock conviction: they rule by an almost divine right and are therefore entitled—indeed, duty-bound—to set the moral tone for the nation.

If we set aside the idea that skin color or ethnic descent is all-determinative, we can see the striking continuity and power of post-Protestant WASP culture. Nearly everyone in Barack Obama's White House has been shaped by old WASP institutions. The president's *consigliere*, Valerie Jarrett, had an international upbringing comparable to that of Henry Adams and went to Stanford. Michelle Obama went to Princeton and Harvard. Our first black president himself is very much the WASP, all the way down to his cool, self-possessed manner and his presumption that he holds the moral high ground. This is not surprising. His mother was a post-Protestant WASP, as were the grandparents who raised him. After a toney progressive prep school in Honolulu founded by Congregationalists, he went to Occidental College, a progressive liberal arts college founded by Presbyterian clergy, transferred to Columbia University, and then attended Harvard Law School. His veneration of his African roots and work as a community organizer reflect the post-Protestant WASP values of diversity and noblesse oblige.

From their elite cultural perch, these post-Protestant WASPs contend with pastors and priests for moral leadership. Preaching a progressive creed based on psychology and a utilitarian philosophy, they promise freedom from traditional sexual norms. This new American identity, that of the secular progressive, is a secure and culturally influential home for Nones. The agnostic elementary school teacher in Des Moines, an eccentric in 1959 who probably kept her views to herself, now participates in post-Protestant WASP confidence and supports its moral and political projects.

The reconstitution of elite WASP culture as post-Protestant and ethnically diverse but intellectually homogeneous is the most important change in American society of the past half-century. It explains the culture wars of recent decades far more effectively than the standard overemphasis of the role of the Religious Right.

Conservative Protestants came to the fore in the 1950s as a potent cultural and political force. In a family feud among white Protestant Americans, they challenged liberal Protestantism's claim to be the Christian conscience of America. At issue was America's future. Would conservative or liberal Protestantism be the leaven that makes us a Christian nation? The 1960s changed a great deal of American culture, but the competition between almost entirely white and mostly Protestant Americans for cultural leadership remained a constant. The Religious Right that emerged in the 1970s gave political muscle to conservative Protestantism, while secular progressivism and identity politics became the vehicle for post-Protestant WASPs in their quest to define our national purpose.

Nobody conducts surveys of post-Protestant WASPs because their very existence contradicts our obsession with race. We refuse to recognize them even as they rule us. The invisibility of the post-Protestant WASPs is a great political advantage, allowing them to oversee identity politics without themselves appearing to be the superordinate social class. Post-Protestant WASPs pose as "inclusive" while practicing a ruthless politics that destroys their opponents, tarred as "extremists" and "bigots." Anyone who has dissented from post-Protestant WASP orthodoxies on a college campus knows how that works.

Despite their telling lack of curiosity about our ruling class, sociologists have studied the political and social attitudes of Nones. What evangelical churchgoers are to the Religious Right, Nones are to the post-Protestant WASP ruling class—the foot soldiers who supply their political muscle.

In 2012 a Pew study reported that 72 percent of Nones supported legalized abortion, compared with 53 percent of the general population, and 73 percent supported same-sex marriage, compared with 48 percent of the public at large. Although the study did not inquire into other issues, I think it's a safe bet that the results would have been similar for doctor-assisted suicide, embryo-destructive research, reproductive technology, legalizing drug use, and censorship of pornography. A survey of the opinions of the trustees of the Metropolitan Museum of Art would very likely predict what Nones as a whole believe about morality, culture, and politics. Taking their marching orders from post-Protestant WASPs, Nones now drive the culture wars. They're the values voters of the twenty-first century.

In *American Grace: How Religion Divides and Unites Us*, Robert Putnam and David Campbell illustrate the political implications of the rise of the Nones. They found that 50 percent of those who say grace before meals identify themselves as Republican, 40 percent as Democrats, and 10 percent as independents. No surprise there. It's common for the media to speak of religious conservatives as the base of the Republican Party. What's striking, however, is the intense partisan loyalty of those who *never* say grace—70 percent of them identify as Democrats and only 20 percent as Republicans.

A breakdown of election results confirms this partisan pattern, which has become more marked in recent years. In 2000, 61 percent of Nones voted for Al Gore. In 2004, 67 percent went for John Kerry. In 2008, 75 percent cast their ballot for Barack Obama, and the same percentage did so again in 2012. These overwhelming majorities suggest that Nones are highly motivated by moral and cultural issues that revolve around their central commitment to the freedom of each individual to define the meaning of life for himself. Under the leadership of post-Protestant WASPs, the Nones are the most dynamic political force in America. This new Moral Majority isn't monolithic, but it's unified, especially in its rejection of the social influence of Christianity.

Such is the current shape of our culture wars. Under the leadership of the post-Protestant WASPs, the Nones go to the polls with a fervor that makes them the secular antithesis of evangelical Christians, who vote for conservative politicians. They collide with the Nones over abortion, gay rights, doctor-assisted suicide, and a range of other issues. But it's useful to dig a little deeper into the cultural differences, because they help us see the strengths and weaknesses of post-Protestant WASP culture.

In a three-year study, *Culture of American Families: A National Survey*, researchers at the University of Virginia found four basic types of family culture, which they call the Faithful, Engaged Progressives, the Detached, and American Dreamers. The latter two cultures largely accept the status quo. Detached parents report a feeling of helplessness. For good or ill, their kids are formed by popular culture. American Dreamers are more positive. They want their children to succeed, but they let society define what counts as success. By contrast, the Faithful and Engaged Progressives raise their children on their own terms, imparting well-formed, confident, and comprehensive worldviews. They are the two family types that have cultural strength and influence.

In this study, 20 percent of American parents are counted among the Faithful, a figure that roughly corresponds to the 25 percent of the population identified as regular churchgoers in other studies. Rejecting the sexual revolution, 68 percent of Faithful parents disagree strongly with the proposition that "sex before marriage is okay if a couple love each other," and 69 percent think contraception should not be made available to teenagers without their parents' approval. Three-quarters reject same-sex marriage.

Mothers among the Faithful are more likely than other mothers to stay at home with their children. The Faithful are much more likely than other parents to "completely agree" that a woman should put family above career, but they also insist with equal vehemence that the same holds for men. Family trumps personal needs and desires. Not surprisingly, the faithful are also hostile to the culture of divorce. A striking 60 percent reject the view that divorce is preferable to sustaining an unhappy marriage, as compared to 16 percent of all other parents. Eighty-eight percent are married, and 74 percent remain in their first marriages.

These families don't adopt the nonjudgmentalism that reigns in Charles Murray's Belmont. They do not conform to the dogmas of our therapeutic age. A resounding 91 percent disagree that "as long as we don't hurt others, we should be able to live however we want," a view that puts them at odds with one of the most important moral principles of post-Protestant WASP culture. Eighty-eight percent think we should guide our behavior by what God or Scripture says. Overall, the Faithful subscribe to Mary Douglas's restricted code, positional control, upholding firm rules and objective moral truths.

The strong consensus among the Faithful about the importance of moral authority gives them cultural power. Faithful parents are not cowed by mass culture. They express confidence in their convictions and are willing to discipline their children to make sure they pass on their religious beliefs and moral values. Two-thirds say that controlling teenagers' access to technology (Internet, social media, cell phones) is *not* a losing battle. They're overwhelmingly more likely than the general population of parents to agree with the statement, "It is my responsibility to help others lead more moral lives." Being censorious or judgmental isn't a sin but an expression of moral concern for others. The Faithful form strong communities, often organized around church and church-related education for their children. They have a place to stand, so they enjoy a high degree of freedom. They're the ones most likely to stand up against progressive educators or to hold views at odds with those promoted by the mainstream media. Because they have a culture, the Faithful can be countercultural.

Engaged Progressive parents are equally committed and equally determined. Accounting for 21 percent of all parents, they are as numerous as the Faithful. There are undoubtedly some liberal Christians among them, but for the most part they are post-Protestant WASPs. They emphasize personal autonomy. More than half subscribe to John Stuart Mill's harm principle, affirming that "as long as we don't hurt others, we should all just live however we want." A supermajority (83 percent) of them agrees that we should be tolerant of "alternative lifestyles."

Engaged Progressives endorse a mobile and plastic view of morality, one attuned to personal needs and differences. Skeptical of traditional authorities, 80 percent of Engaged Progressive parents say they wouldn't appeal to Scripture or religion in guiding the moral development of their children. They tend to reject spanking, with a third of them regarding spanking as always wrong—a reliable predictor, in my experience, of the whole range of progressive views. Following Mary Douglas's enhanced code, personal control mode of social authority, they want their kids to be fair-minded, caring, and nonjudgmental. They seek a therapeutic culture in which people are affirmed and supported in their personal journeys.

Engaged Progressives say that divorce is preferable to an unhappy marriage, but like the denizens of Charles Murray's Belmont, they don't practice what they preach. They are almost as likely to remain married, in fact, as the Faithful. They are just as likely to eat meals with their children, and Engaged Progressive mothers with preschool kids are nearly as likely to stay at home with them as their Faithful counterparts. They may be less enthusiastic about moral authority than the Faithful, or at least sound as though they are, but they're no less committed to maintaining their families and serving the needs of their kids. Almost all (93 percent) say that they invest a great deal of effort in shaping the moral character of their children. Their ideology may be permissive, but their actual practice conforms to many old-fashioned values that give them strong families. Engaged Progressives have succeeded in reinventing themselves, shedding both Christianity and an ethnically based sense of identity while sustaining a strong marriage and family culture. They have social capital that they pass along to their kids.

Given the differences in family cultures, it's not surprising that the Faithful and Engaged Progressives clash in the voting booth. The Faithful make up the socially conservative base of the Republican Party. Engaged Progressives are the socially progressive base of the Democratic Party—they favor it by a four-to-one margin— a party the post-Protestant WASP elites control through donations and as members of the media.

We've all read about the Religious Right. Recently, pollsters have become aware of the political influence of the Nones. More subtle than the political collisions of these two groups, however, is their clash over social institutions. The standard story of cultural conflict in America has conservative Christians defending established forms of social authority, while Progressives see themselves as challenging established norms and institutions, a self-assessment that the media accept at face value. The reality is the opposite. The counter-culturalism of the Faithful gives them an independent spirit. The committed core of Christians in America increasingly lives on the peripheries of cultural and institutional power. The Engaged Progressives, in command of civic institutions, are the establishmentarians.

A HOLLOW STRENGTH

Establishments always seem impregnable, but we shouldn't overestimate the strength of post-Protestant WASP culture. Yes of course, control of institutions like Stanford and Princeton or the *Washington Post* and the *New York Times* allows post-Protestant WASPs to define themselves and their worldview as "mainstream." Dissenters, by definition outside the mainstream, are thus dismissed as extremists rather than engaged in argument. But with establishment status comes responsibility, and with responsibility comes liability. When people become disgruntled with the status quo, they blame the establishment. When the mainstream fails, post-Protestant WASPs and their worldview are discredited.

This book is essentially an argument that post-Protestant WASP culture is failing, that it promises freedom, but delivers tyranny. It may work well for the top end of society, but it's hell on the weak and vulnerable. It makes a fuss about diversity but can't deliver solidarity. Its false view of freedom undermines the authority of the two institutions that can limit government: marriage and the church. Its this-worldly focus distracts us from the higher things that give us a firm place to stand and from the higher loves that make us free.

This failure can be hard to see. The path from nonjudgmentalism, the cardinal virtue of post-Protestant WASP culture, to the deterioration of the condition of the poor is indirect. Mary Douglas uses the terms of social science to describe the disorientation brought about by the open-ended, therapeutic morality favored by the upper classes, but her description illuminates rather than proves, and even the illumination is only partial. The same goes for my exposition of the connection between a weakening culture of marriage and the expansion of government. It may resonate with readers, but that's not the same as proof.

But the social dysfunction Robert Putnam describes in *Our Kids* and the growing divide between rich and poor that Charles Murray documents in *Coming Apart* are easy to see. Whether we call the problem income inequality, an opportunity gap, or declining social capital, it's clear that our society is not healthy. The life expectancy of a white woman without a high school degree declined by five years between 1990 and 2010, an indication of a shocking cultural collapse. It's a sign of the perversion of our age that we ignore it.

We can argue about causes of our society's troubles. Some blame "financial capitalism," others technology, and still others the sexual revolution. But the American financial system is not the creation of evangelical pastors in Texas. Catholic bishops do not run our cities' failing public schools. Christianity did not produce the hookup culture that has made sexual assault a hazard of college life. These institutions are dominated by the post-Protestant WASP establishment, which is also responsible for our popular music, movies, and television. Today's regime is a secular progressive one, which is to say a post-Protestant WASP regime.

My point right now is not that our system exploits the weak and rewards the powerful—though it does—but that what looks like an invincible establishment is vulnerable, very vulnerable. In places like New Hampshire, there has been a rise in deaths from drug overdoses, a trend that, along with others, discredits today's cultural regime. At some point, people will notice what the post-Protestant WASPs have done. They have built a culture that suits college graduates like themselves while disorienting everyone else. In fact, given the sincere moral purpose that animates most post-Protestant WASPs, they will start to have their own misgivings, at which point the Christian leaven will go to work on the lump.

A reprise of Christendom is unlikely, but a religious counter-culture unimaginable fifty years ago has emerged in America. Though it sometimes expresses anger and despair over what has happened to our society, it is fundamentally confident, even hopeful. This religious counterculture, you see, is not really *counter*. We Christians recognize the value of the secular and the importance of man's temporal welfare, but soulcraft is more important than statecraft. Our ambition is not to become the next establishment but to influence, directly and indirectly, the moral and spiritual outlook of the current one, turning it in directions that promote wellbeing for everyone, not just those who live in Belmont.

Exercising that influence sometimes means being forceful. Having put on the "whole armor of God," we are called to contend "against the principalities, against the powers, against the world rulers of this present darkness" (Ephesians 6:11–12). All of us feel in our bones that a great deal is at stake. We can't simply step aside. We owe our neighbors, Christian or not, a faithful witness to the truth, even if it provokes controversy. We follow a Lord who said, "I have not come to bring peace, but a sword" (Matthew 10:34).

All true! But the "armor of God" includes the "equipment of the gospel of peace" (Ephesians 6:15). Christians are called not to win debates and elections but to build a civilization of love—never an easy task, certainly not today. In their crusade for inclusiveness, tolerance, and diversity, the Nones have taken a battering ram to traditional mores, furiously denouncing anyone who does not agree with them. It is difficult not to respond to such distilled partisanship without partisanship of one's own.

Our partisanship, however, need not echo the politically correct intolerance that gives the post-Protestant WASP universities such a bad reputation. Fortunately, for the most part it doesn't. The Catholic University of America is far more ideologically diverse than any state university because the awareness that one is limited by original sin encourages a certain intellectual humility. The command to love your enemies promotes unity more effectively than the haughty conviction that you're on the right side of history.

St. Paul tells us to speak the truth in love (Ephesians 4:15), but the Bible also offers practical guidance in civility, a virtue Christians should bring to the public square. Above all there's the Golden Rule: Do unto others as you would have them do unto you (Matthew 7:12). One of the most destructive tactics of post-Protestant WASP polemics—deployed with particular fervor in the debate over same-sex marriage—is recklessly impugning the motives of one's opponents. The Golden Rule enjoins us to treat others as morally committed fellow citizens who also seek to promote the common good.

St. Paul exhorted the Christians of Rome to refrain from doing evil for the sake of a greater good (Romans 3:8). A great deal is at stake in our political debates, and civility does not prevent us from employing forceful words and images when necessary. Nevertheless, we need to discipline our public witness. Let us shun rhetorical victories that rely on distortions or half-truths. Prevarication produces an atmosphere of distrust. We should likewise face up to the implications of our own positions. One of the most powerful components of the prolife movement is its crisis-pregnancy centers, which represent an honest recognition of the serious difficulties attending most personal decisions about abortion.

Jesus's declaration that his kingdom is not of this world (John 18:36) fortifies the Christian commitment to civility. Christ's lordship makes a difference in the world, which is why we rightly engage in the public square. But his kingdom is not of this world. Moral truths are at stake, but not our souls. We are right to concern ourselves with our nation's future, but because our citizenship is ultimately in heaven, not earth, that concern is not fraught with ultimate significance.

By contrast, our secular establishment talks a great deal about tolerance, or its postmodern version, inclusivity. But since post-Protestant WASP culture lacks a transcendent horizon, politics is its be-all and end-all. The stakes thus raised, "politically correct" views become sacred dogma, dissent becomes heresy. This sacralization of the political is nothing new. It has characterized modern politics whenever faith in God above has been replaced by faith in History, Destiny, or Progress. Today's theocrats are not Christians. They are the Nones, whose political views are their highest loyalties.

The proper interplay of Christian political commitment and the awareness of our transcendent destiny is suggested in Jesus's admonition to be "wise as serpents and innocent as doves" (Matthew 10:16). It's no sin against civility to be serpent-wise about what it takes to win in political debates. Sometimes we need to enter into coalitions, downplaying disagreements with allies. Even though the Democratic and Republican Parties are imperfect vehicles for a consistent vision of the common good, we can still make use of them. Let's avoid a false purism. It would be political Pharisaism to refuse to pollute oneself with the realities of public life in a fallen world.

But we can't *only* be wise as serpents. A healthy political culture needs a spirit of innocence as well. Christians must speak the truth even if it is politically inexpedient. Knowing that Christ already reigns, we can attain a holy indifference, borne of a higher love rather than the cynical indifference of moral relativism or materialism. A superordinate power that oversees public life allows us to speak the truth in season and out of season with the confidence that, even when our political voices are ineffective, they can leaven the future. This spirit of engagement—articulate and confident, not angry or shrill—encourages a renewal of solidarity. It allows us to cherish what we hold in common, however spirited our disagreements. Civility should not be confused with conflict-avoidant "niceness."

The Christian faith thus encourages hospitality. In political debate, we should invite others to join our common life, even the stranger and sojourner, addressing the most existentially potent topics—God, salvation, the meaning of history—Jews speaking as Jews, Muslims as Muslims, Marxists as Marxists, Christians as Christians. We don't need to police one another's arguments.

Post-Protestant WASPs lack this hospitality and so limit discussion to secular liberal categories. In their institutions, freedom is diminished. Speech is carefully monitored and corrected. We're told what pronouns to use, or not, and are subjected to an ever-changing etiquette for speaking about sex and sexual orientation. Certain topics and points of view get censured. There is a far greater range of moral and political opinion in American churches than in a typical newsroom or editorial board. When we have our eyes on higher things, we're able to be more generous about our disagreements about how to address lower things.

America needs this spirit of hospitality. Divided by globalization and increasing cultural differences, we strain to maintain solidarity. Secular progressives' insistence that those who disagree with them stand in the way of progress is profoundly uncivil, for such rhetoric amounts to demanding submission to their inevitable triumph. This is not an invitation to shared citizenship but the imposition of servitude. Perhaps I'm unreasonably optimistic (a very American trait), but I persevere in my conviction that most Americans, including those in power, want a culture of hospitality and freedom, not denunciation and servitude. They may not become Christians, but they just might find themselves newly grateful for a renewal of Christian influence on society.

AFTERWORD

I t's easy to be demoralized. Many powerful forces want to make us "dhimmis," the Muslim term for non-Muslims who are tolerated as long as they don't evangelize or challenge the supremacy of Islam. There are political dimensions to this pressure, such as the U.S. Health and Human Services Department's contraceptive mandate, an exercise of executive power to compel participation in one of the central practices of the Sexual Revolution, and the official harassment of Gordon College because of its biblical policies on sexual morality. As I write, the Obama administration is considering a reversal of the policy of exempting religious organizations from nondiscrimination rules that otherwise apply to organizations that receive government grants—the necessary first step toward forcing their conformity with today's sexual orthodoxies.

We can defend our freedoms with the political and legal means available. I'm guardedly optimistic. Recent Supreme Court decisions have been solicitous of religious liberty. But there is a danger greater than oppressive and unjust laws. Scholars of the Islamic world coined the term "dhimmitude" to describe the ways non-Muslims internalized their subordination in regions dominated by Islam, accepting it as normal and natural. We too are in danger of dhimmitude, an internalized submission to the progressives' claim that they control the future, a mentality based on the illusion that worldly powers are history's master and that they set the ultimate conditions for our freedom. The seductions of this illusion are powerful, but historical reality testifies otherwise.

My wife is Jewish. Her ancestors lived for generations in the contested borderlands of Poland and Russia. Always vulnerable, they never enjoyed political freedom. Often persecuted, sometimes killed, they endured. That seems like a small thing, but it is not. Today the Polish and Russian aristocratic regimes that once dominated them are gone. And what of the Soviet Union, the Worker's Paradise that purported to transcend all religion? What of the Thousand-Year Reich that imagined it could wipe Judaism from the face of the earth? They are dust, just like the Roman Empire that razed the city of Jerusalem, just like the medieval monarchies that drove Jews eastward into Poland and Russia centuries ago.

Unlike these influential and powerful civilizations, institutions, and ideologies, Judaism endures. The Torah is still read in the synagogue. It turns out that over those long and difficult centuries, only Jews had a future—and they still have a future.

The same holds for Christianity. Along with the synagogue, the church is the only surviving institution from antiquity. St. Paul is a living voice for us, as are St. Athanasius, St. Augustine, and countless others. In fact, apart from a handful of monarchies, which persist only in considerably modified forms, and the universities, the church and synagogue are the only surviving medieval institutions, or for that matter the only ones left from the early modern era.

The administrative state, democratic constitutions, and the limited liability corporation are modern inventions. Under the control of post-Protestant WASPs, who are more shaped by these powerful modern institutions than they realize or admit, they seek to absorb all social reality into themselves. Marriage is now a creature of the courts, not the pre-political institution it was from the beginnings of recorded history. The university, one of the great achievements of the Middle Ages, is being subsumed into the techno-bureaucratic logic of our era. Only religious institutions endure on their own terms. They do not depend on secular authorities for authorization, licensing, or accreditation, as Christians in China remind us. They are free.

Yes, wealth seduces. Governments regulate, coerce, and punish. It has always been so. But neither wealth nor political power has created anything that has lasted. By contrast, over the long

ACKNOWLEDGMENTS

A great deal of this book incorporates ideas, themes, and analysis put forward in the pages of *First Things*. It's an honor to serve as editor of that fine journal of religion and public life, and I'm indebted to the founder of *First Things*, Richard John Neuhaus. He was determined to speak with both a public and Christian voice—a high standard.

Editors need editors, and I'd like to thank mine. Mark Bauerlein, David Mills, and Matthew Schmitz challenged and refined my thinking as I struggled to find my voice in my monthly column in *First Things*, "The Public Square." Without them I would not have been able to write this book. Tom Spence took hold of the manuscript and banged it into shape, gently cutting what needed to be cut and reformulating my tangled sentences.

Finally, a word of gratitude for my friends in Omaha, Nebraska: you helped me see what's lasting and true in the American dream.

INDEX